More Techniques of
DEEP Clearing
How to Release Stress and Charge from Mind, Heart and Body

By Rolf Dane

and Ability Press, Copenhagen, Denmark
Email, Author: Rolf_Dane@yahoo.com
Bookstore: Lulu.com att. Rolf Dane

ISBN: 978-87-999547-4-2 (Print edition)

ISBN 978-87-999547-4-2

9 788799 954742

ISBN: 978-87-999547-5-9 (PDF edition)

ISBN: 978-87-999547-6-6 (ePub/Kindle edition)

These publications and more are available
at our bookstore at: Lulu.com, att. Rolf Dane

Table of Content

Author's Foreword

This publication "More Techniques of DEEP Clearing" is a follow-up on our first book on the subject, "DEEP Clearing – Releasing the Power of Your Mind". In this present publication we bring some new and old techniques. New techniques are Deep Awareness and Aspect Clearing that was developed in 2017 – 18. In 2019 we ran into a similar technique developed independently by Marc Rüedi. We did the training with Marc in his '4-Stage4 Release Rundown' and received extensive facilitation from him. We have included our write-up of Mr. Rüedi's technique in this publication.

Of 'old' techniques we here publish DEEP Character Clearing for the first time. It was our original research project and technique going back to 2005 but the publishing of the method was delayed again and again as it remained in pilot project mode. We have still delivered it to selected students as part of the pilot project.

Chapter 16 is by Heidrun Beer. It describes a technique called DEEP Space Clearing. This technique is still in the pilot phase but has produced some spectacular successes so we have included it here. Feedback from clearers using this technique is welcome as is feedback in general.

In the appendix you will likewise find two already published techniques, 'DEEP Subject Clearing' and 'DEEP Incident Clearing, Light'. These are very useful techniques covered fully in the first book. But we have included them in short form here as to make it a complete handbook in practical use.

Since the first publication of our first book in 2013 we have learned a lot. What we learned resulted in two updates of the original book, 2015 and 2019. Still, there was more to be discovered and be reported and this is done with this publication.

Rolf Dane,
Copenhagen, April 22, 2020

The 2024 edition is identical to the 2020 edition. The only difference is that it is released as trade edition with its own ISBN and in three versions an eBook version (Kindle/ePub), a PDF version and a print version.

Copenhagen, October 14, 2024

Illustrated Intro to DAC

In Deep Awareness and Aspect Clearing (DAC) we take up any issue known from therapy and self-development and release related reactive thoughts, emotions, sensations and other subtle energies in body and mind. In this way the whole issue is cleared up. It is emptied for charge and irrationality. The table below gives a quick overview.

Emotional Activities

Emotions are traditionally seated in the heart. But as you can see from scientific study brought in the appendix, they spread throughout the body. We have a range of well-known and named emotions, such as apathy, fear, anger, boredom and joy. But beyond that there is a near infinity of *feelings* that are hard to describe but still very meaningful.

In *Deep Awareness and Aspect Clearing* we see emotions and feelings as guiding systems. They tell us important things about ourselves, about other people and situations in general – danger, neutral, opportunity, etc.

Feelings and emotions can however take over if ignored for a long time. They may take control over our mental activities and our body. Sometimes this can cause hell.

Deep Awareness and Aspect Clearing addresses the whole range of emotions and feelings and restores our emotional life to being a reliable guiding system and a life quality.

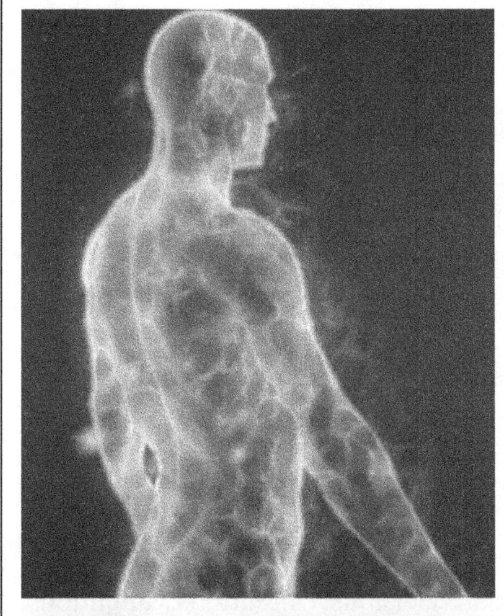

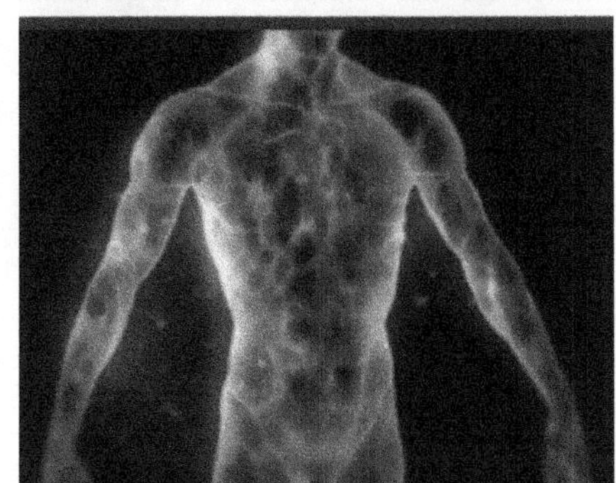

Body Activities (Physical Activity and Sensations)

The person's physical energies and body sensations are controlling and monitoring the body. Such energies can be sensed in the muscles and tissues in the activated parts - both as muscle activities (including impulses) and sensations.

Physical activity can be action and efforts, tensions, a state of rest, movements and whole routines.

There is a range of body sensations such as: pain, hunger, fullness, soreness, pressure, exhaustion, a feeling of relaxation and wellness, etc.

Body activities also include what is called *body language*, consisting of posture, tensions, position of limbs, hands and head, facial expression and so on.

How we feel in the body obviously affects our sense of wellbeing and energy level in general. The energies and sensations that exist in the body at any given moment are of course partly due to our immediate or recent physical activity and our health. But many negative body sensations are rooted in what we call *Body Memories* stemming from long gone periods of physical, emotional and mental stress.

Such tensions can be located and relieved with Deep Awareness and Aspect Clearing.

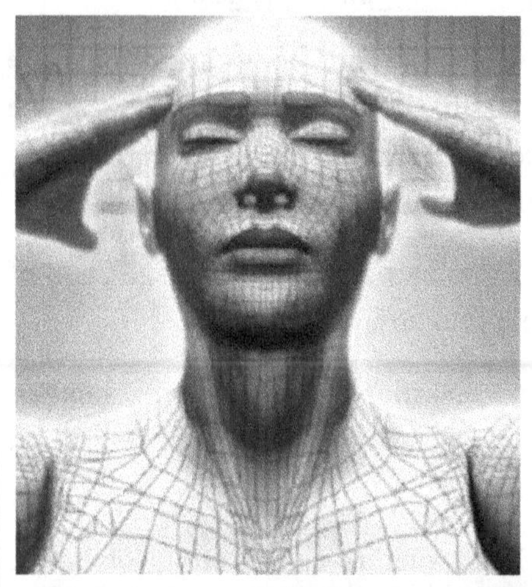

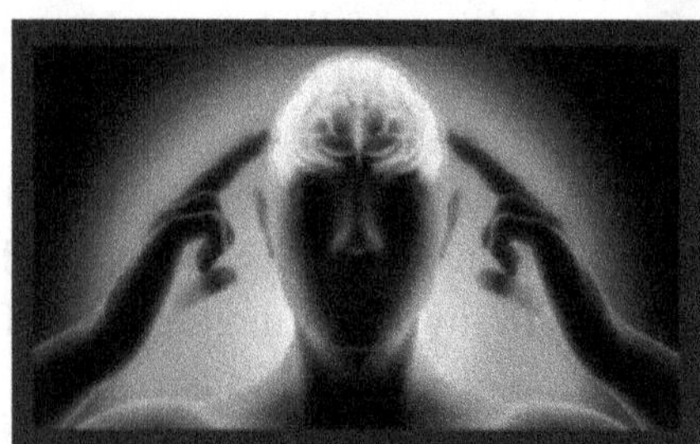

Mental Activities

Mental activities, such as thoughts, decisions, intentions and attentions, rational thinking, etc., are traditionally seated in the head. They include the use of language – be it written or verbal descriptions and messages sent and received.

Science shows they are concentrated in the head and brain, especially in the prefrontal cortex ('the Executive brain').

We may add that *you as a spiritual being are in control of the brain.* You *can* be in control of your attentions, intentions, thoughts and decisions.

Mental energies: thoughts, decisions, intentions, attentions, etc. may trigger responses in emotions and body. They may trigger negative or burdening reactions and sometimes keep them in suspense for a long of time.

In Deep Awareness and Aspect Clearing *we look into the interaction between head, heart and body and bring out and neutralize the reactive thoughts that may cause unnecessary distress and hardship.*

Deep Awareness and Aspect Clearing (DAC)

In *Deep Awareness and Aspect Clearing* we have the person contact these subtle energies and we do techniques and exercises with them.

It may take a little time (a minute or so) to contact these subtle energies that tend to take over in stressful situations. Especially emotional energies and body energies (including sensations) are prone to be out of control in many situations.

We have the person give a subjective description of the inner experience. Like, *"How does it feel in the body? Can you describe that in words?"*

We then find a symbol, a 'thing' or image that would represent that.

Now we do a series of techniques and exercises that enable the person to get familiar with, release or gain control over these subtle energies. Doing this will eliminate negative and out of control factors. These factors sometimes seem so strange to us that they may be seen as destiny, curses, haunting spirits, being possessed, or sub-personalities.

The end-result of doing Deep Awareness and Aspect Clearing *is a harmonic state: emotionally, mentally and physically. There are no more stray sub-personalities or attachments that mysteriously pull you in the wrong direction. You are in control of your destiny. It is a state of integrity where you remain balanced and your own good self – even under trying circumstances.*

Chapter 1
DEEP Awareness and Aspect Clearing

By Rolf Dane (June 4, 2018, updated March 19, 2020.)

Name: Deep Awareness and Aspect Clearing; also called DAC or Aspect Clearing.

In Deep Awareness and Aspect Clearing we address the subconscious and unconscious minds in a new way.

We have found that our 'bodies' are holding certain mental energies and a "knowing" (intuitive knowledge) that correspond to the subconscious and unconscious minds. The content is organized in entities or packages. The packages can be perceived directly as an intuitive feeling and "knowing" in what seems to be the body. Our process of perceiving this is called ***Deep Awareness****. The negative effects of these packages can be processed using various techniques based on perception and communication. We call the packages* ***'Aspects'****. At its core, Aspect Clearing develops our ability to perceive, accept and "own" these subtle energies and their "knowing" and to transform, integrate or release them through various techniques. We bring burdensome subconscious content into the bright light of our consciousness where we now can see clearly what is real and important – and what is delusion or counter-productive, distorted ideas regarding our condition and perception of reality.*

In combining new research and the study of other methods with our earlier research and techniques of ***DEEP Clearing (*1)*** *we have, we think, come up with a unique and powerful self-development method. DAC is relatively easy to learn and very effective when dealing with case-problems that earlier methods couldn't fully crack.*

Getting Started

First you pick an issue, something that bothers you (or your client) or something you recall that bothered you in the past. It can be an incident, a body condition, a relationship, stress, a block, such as a writer's or speaker's block, back-offs from certain persons or situations, an inability, a mystery, a hang-up, and many other things. In short: any traditional problem and issue known from therapy and self-development.

Deep Awareness (*2)

You apply Deep Awareness and look into your body – mainly chest, heart and throat region. But other areas can attract attention, especially belly and abdomen. The neck and physical head (as different from mind) are sometimes in play. Something will attract your attention. You look for something to form – you do not pick thoughts, earlier conclusions or theories/explanations. Not even reactions and emotions/ feelings you already know and have had dozens of times in relation to the subject. You may of course start there but you are after the Deep Awareness.

We are after a new intuitive feel of the subject – what we call a Deep Awareness. This feel is the telltale sign of the Aspect (*3) (Aspect: the part of us holding the issue, such as an energy frequency, a mental mass or sub-personality). This is what you want to address. You accept it as a part of you – but separate from your core. You may say: "A part of me is [afraid of spiders]" Then say "Hello!" to that part. Sit and sense it for a moment. Notice **where it is located** and give it some room. (This has since been expanded to the formal Dialogue step.) The whole pursuit of Deep Aspect Clearing is to get to know this part of you; get in communication with it, allow it to express itself and handle it in different ways – to a point where it no longer bothers you. It has either been integrated into your core personality; or it has been inspected and resolved as it was an isolated part that worked against your wellbeing.

Perception Step

One way to get to know about the obscure phenomena and energies roaming in your body and system is to describe them as you see them. In the Perception Step we assume an external and objective viewpoint and from there we examine the potential Aspect. We try to describe the phenomena as an objective observer would. This action gets the observation and communication going. The obscure energies begin to take form. We now have a 'Something', a part; but we need it in a form where we can see it as an object of sorts, a 'thing'. We need a good label for it.

Note: As we go further down the procedure we will even discover that 'the thing' *seems* to be alive. It has a personality of its own.

Getting the Aspect Expressed – The Item

You work back and forth in order to get the part, the Aspect expressed. On the one side you have these energetic phenomena in body and mind; on the other side you probably have questions like, "what is this?" Often it's just a "something"; like 'a sore something' 'an angry something', etc. Just an energy or feeling in the body. Sometimes it can appear to be a character (a part, a viewpoint). As you grabble with it, it can appear or be expressed as a shape or picture – often of symbolic character. Examples of Items of different Aspects would be: a fearful face; an object, such as a fried brain, a crooked tree, a shiny building, a totem pole with known faces, etc.; a traditional symbol, such as a cross, a star, a sun, a sword, etc. – all in a unique rendition; it can be a human identity – friend or enemy; an animal, such as the family dog, a duck, a huge spider, a happy bear, etc. Or it can simply be an energy mass in the body – a stiff neck, a blob of clay in the chest, heavy lead in the abdomen, a nervous stomach, and so on. The exercise here is to get this sorted out. Obviously, the great variety above would not apply to one Aspect but maybe something you could encounter over time when doing many Aspects and many hours of DAC. Usually it comes down to a few possibilities in relation to one Deep Awareness phenomenon.

Whatever comes up, and what you get will be something very personal and sometimes weird, you check a possible Item (the symbol) against your Deep Awareness; the intuitive body-feel, the sensing of this cloudy and obscure area and feeling that seems to *reside in your body and energy-systems – not in your mind*.

Looking for it in the body rather than the mind is an important point. *The Aspect does not reside in what we normally understand by mind*: our thoughts, explanations, conclusions, suppositions, deductions, etc. You look past already known material and get a completely fresh and direct perception of the energy or biofield (aura) emanating from and surrounding the issue. This direct perception may sometimes first be possible after some discussion back and forth, of course. If so, take the discussion and guide the person towards the Deep Awareness and the Aspect.

Finding the Right Item

You now have this firsthand impression. What we want to arrive at is a specific, a single representation of it. In that way it becomes a concrete 'thing' that we can use in our DAC techniques. As described above, you go back and forth between the Deep Awareness you sensed in the body and the possible expression/symbol for it until it feels just right. You should experience a moment of relief, a smile or laughter; a relaxation in your body – an 'Ah Ha! Moment'. Now you have got it. It's something the Aspect and you both feel comfortable about. You feel it's just right and with very good indicators. That's your Item!

Kathy McGuire (of Creative Edge Focusing) puts it this way: "You go back and forth between the intuition of your right brain and the more rational thinking of your left brain."

In DEEP we would say, you go between your body-experience and its intuition and the energetic and emotional content on the one hand – and your head/mind, where language, pictures, and the naming of things take place, on the other hand. This whole process of finding the Item takes time. Just getting the cloudy or obscure feeling of the Aspect using Deep Awareness can take up to a couple of minutes. (The question, "How is the weather in there?" is sometimes useful.) But you need to spend whatever time is necessary on this step, finding the right Item. This is an absolute prerequisite for the whole procedure going forward successfully! Basically you are getting an answer to "What are you?" or "What can we call this?" You want something that will represent the Aspect to you personally. Once it is successful you have transformed the obscure area to a 'thing', a mental object that you can move around and communicate with. And, as said, you will soon discover it is not just 'a thing' – it is alive!

Aspects Have a Life of their Own

Apparently, we store our experiences, our "gut reactions and feelings", our intuitions about things in the body. It seems to be stored as information in the electro-magnetic field that surrounds and permeates the physical body. Today this, the traditional aura, is called The Biofield in cutting edge science. This field can be measured electronically, using various electronic instruments (*5). This is, it could be said, the seat for our subconscious and unconscious minds.

As described in the DEEP book, we make complex Emotional Markers (set emotional reactions) as shortcuts for dealing with complex circumstances. In daily language this is called Likes and Dislikes or Bypass Reactions (reactive responses). In DAC we dig them up, find out what they mean and discharge the burdensome ones that pull us in the wrong direction.

What we find is "alive". Each Aspect has a life of its own. It has a unique set of experiences and life qualities. This should also prepare us for seeing changes in emotions/feelings and expression within the Aspect as we go along with the processing of it. Fear may change to anger. An intention to attack may change to an intention to befriend. The Aspect has emotions/feelings, intentions, impulses, imagery and points of view; but all thoroughly repressed and ignored in normal living. In situations we are uncomfortable about, we talk about, "I had this feeling... about it, but I ignored it and got myself in trouble." That is the intuitive feel at work. The type of awareness we explore.

Aspects for Everything

We find Deep Awarenesses and Aspects related to just about anything. To mannerisms, obsessive thoughts, hang-ups in past incidents and relationships; procrastinations and activity blocks; body-problems; fears; losing one's temper, compulsions, mysteries – and down through the catalogue of unwanted feelings, thoughts, behaviors, dependencies, shortcomings, and body conditions. We also find Aspects for happy events and relationships that should be cherished. We are not saying that DAC is a cure-all method for all the negative phenomena. But finding the Aspect-side of unwanted conditions enables us to see the situation from a new and very personal perspective. It can be the key that opens the door to relieve much pain and suffering.

Working with the Aspects

Once we have formulated the Aspect (a beingness or a 'something') into an Item (a significance, a naming) we have something to work with. We have found out what to call it. The Deep Awareness has been transformed into an Aspect and then an Item. Whatever we got: a 'something', an expression, a scene, a character, an animal, a plant, an object, a body posture or movement, an energy mass in the body, etc., we can now go ahead. We bring it out of oblivion using the techniques of *Deep Awareness and Aspect Clearing* and discharge and resolve it. The exact procedures and techniques are the subject of other writings in this series.

But we can say this much: The first technique used, after identifying the energetic phenomena, the potential Aspect, has to do with perceiving it as detailed as we can (the Perception step). Even though, to some, the potential Aspect may seem as pure imagination, the Perception step usually gives some very definite answers. So it seems that we simply are dealing with a finer reality than the physical world. We are dealing with the reality of our inner world; the world from where and through which we experience and react to the environment.

Multiple Aspects

There may be many Aspects connected to important issues, say, a charged relationship. Each Aspect is a 'soul-fragment', a 'creature', an 'entity', an 'isolated part of us' that had a certain mission; a little circuit or obsession of sorts. We are completing that mission and the "ice sculpture" will transform and melt and return to the sea of our inner resources. The Aspect integrates with your own beingness and energy field – or it simply releases and blows. It existed as an irregular ridge or vortex in the biofield; a little mental circuit repeating over and over the same uneasy or irrational thought, emotion or behavior. Yet we tried to keep it out of sight by suppressing it. Like an upset child it was making a lot of noise and pulling you in the wrong direction. Now it has been reintegrated into your biofield and energy body as a fully functional family member and available resource. It's adding to, not subtracting from, your overall way of being, and your natural power; your integrity, your authentic self. ¤

Notes, Chapter One

(*1) DEEP Clearing is a self-development method, fully described in the book "DEEP Clearing, Releasing the Power of Your Mind." It is dealing with the D.E.E.P. energies of the human mind and body. By the D.E.E.P. energies we mean the human energies that animate body, mind and relationships. D.E.E.P. is an abbreviation that stands for **Decisions** (mental level); **Emotions** (heart level); **Efforts** (body level); and **Polarities** or **Points of view** (the interpersonal level).)

(*2) Using **Deep Awareness** means you are looking directly into the biofield of the body and the subconscious mind to find the spontaneous reaction. Through quiet and mindful contemplation of your bodily felt reaction you can penetrate below what is usually available to you. It may take a little time to develop. You are after what Eugene Gendlin calls 'The Felt Sense' in his book 'Focusing'. It's the intuitive sense in the body, the "knowing", related to a condition or issue.

We are, of course, mainly addressing Aspects that seem irrational and work against our well-being. We may take up positive Aspects as well and simply validate and cherish them as being positive and vital qualities in our lives.

Note: It is related to what we call an Emotional Marker (p. 87 in the DEEP Clearing book). "Our Likes and Dislikes", you could say. The approach here is however different. In Aspect Clearing the content of the markers take center stage. The 'Emotional Markers' are the very 'Aspects' or 'entities' we are communicating with, examining and liberating you could say.

(*3) Aspect is our word for what we are looking for. Elsewhere it is called sub-personalities, parts, entities, characters, identities, attached beings, aspects, soul-fragments, inner children, disembodied souls, valences, mental circuits, internal voices, inner critic, body thetans, personas – the list goes on. In DEEP we have called them Points of View, Perspectives, Polarities, Characters and Identities. In the various relevant subjects they have been explained in many ways. From being devils, haunting ghosts or traumatized 'dead' spirits, to being walled off sub-personalities, to being short-circuits in the brain. In some modalities they are treated like 'possessions of evil or dead spirits'. We find this approach counter-productive. Most of what we encounter is of our own making: repressed emotions, reactions, energy ridges and imagery that appear to have a life of their own. Thus we get these walled off sub-personalities that simply need to be reintegrated. Intentions and imprints from other outside beings (like family members) may be part of the mix. Occasionally we do encounter dead spirits that need to be taken up. They won't reintegrate but blow off when properly addressed. Usually they attach to the person due to identical frequencies and issues existing on both sides. They need special attention when encountered. But it is important to check if the person also can find their own, 'juicy' Aspects that attracted these 'creatures' or entities. By 'Juicy' we mean a quality of aliveness, such as emotions, feelings and intentions, etc. – the D.E.E.P. energies explained above.

The beauty of DAC is that we can treat all these Aspects – separate Beings, inexplicable ridges of energy, imagery and sub-personalities – simply as 'viewpoints' or identities, without presuppositions about their origin or their possible traumatic history. We do not use explanations from cosmology, Spiritism, or brain-physiology. We simply address what we find here and now as Aspects, using perception and communication, and take it from there.

So in DAC we deal with what we call Aspects. They are slightly different from, a sub-category of, the more general 'Points of View'. And Aspects can also appear to be 'things' with certain properties not related to being alive. What we are looking for resides in the body, the torso or trunk, as the main rule. They may, however, reside anywhere in our immediate space including limbs, head and around the body – in our biofield in other words. They may reside in the physical head as feelings, sensations – or maybe as mental shapes or objects – not reasons or explanations. *In practice this is an all-important difference.* They are not in the mind; they are in the biofield (the physical body's electro-magnetic field). That's our remote storage we take for granted as a fully integrated part of our beingness and character. They are a much more intimate part of how we see ourselves and our sense of 'Who we are' – than the usual content of the mind is. This intimacy is reflected in daily language. We say, for instance, "I *am* afraid of spiders", not, "An Aspect of me is afraid of spiders." If we could just make that distinction (as Ann Weiser Cornell points out) life would be much easier to deal with.

(*4) In DEEP Incident Clearing we were very interested in 'What Happened?' – All the nitty gritty details of 'who did what' and our own and others' actions and reactions in the incident.

In DAC our approach is different. We assume that all major incidents that have presented themselves are handled. What is left on the case are elements and energies, etc. that have a definite effect on the case but are untraceable in terms of history. So instead of getting lost in an impossible attempt to sort out the history, that often leads to inventing likely or unlikely scenarios, we simply deal with the here and now, the energies and DEEP elements that actually impact the case in present time. We take control of these elements and discharge them in the Now. Our overall goal is to integrate or release these phenomena. It is to be cause over our mental landscape – to be cause over our own mental matter, energy, space and time. This can at this point best be accomplished by a causative attitude. In DAC there is a receptive phase: finding the Aspect and Item and describing it – and a causative phase: taking control over the Aspect in a caring and mindful way. We lift the repression so the tensions and energies can complete their course and life cycles in present time. During the DAC Techniques all the small vectors and frequencies in the Aspect will sizzle and fizzle in all directions and either be integrated or released. Once that has happened the Aspect has been handled and we can simply move on.

This does not mean that traumatic and stressful incidents are completely ignored. DAC may uncover 'new' live and distinct incidents and the sensible thing to do is to address them with DEEP Incident Clearing. Other situations may occur as well that call for the use of a variety of tools and techniques contained in DEEP Clearing.

Origins of DAC

The sources we are getting inspiration from include: our own DEEP Viewpoint Clearing and DEEP Character Clearing; Applied Metapsychology (Frank A. Gerbode); Focusing (Eugene Gendlin); Internal Family Systems (Richard Swartz and Jay Early); Internal Relationship Focusing (Ann Weiser Cornell and Barbara McGavin); Creative Edge Focusing (Kathy McGuire); NOTs Processing (L. Ron Hubbard); Excalibur (Bill Robertson).

March 2020 edition: We have since 1st edition studied Marc Rüedi's Science of Releasing and that led to some corrections in the basic running of DEEP packages and to better questions in untangling the Thought level.

We got a substantial help from Stephen Wolinsky (of Quantum Psychology) in smoothing out procedures.

(*5) We have found supporting scientific evidence in HeartMath (Doc Childre) and Biofield Tuning (Eileen McKusick). Various other methods to measure and map the biofield have been inspirational but not crucial (Thornton Streeter's Biofield Viewer; research done with Squid Magnetometers and Gas Discharge Visualization).

Also Mindfulness and other forms of meditation have been inspirational and are relevant. The person doing Aspect Clearing, whether solo or as a client, should assume the role of 'Mindful Self', an attitude of detached, interested and curios observer of the phenomena he/she contacts and processes. As Marc Rüedi points out in his material, Lester Levinson's Releasing (also known as the Sedona Method) is very relevant. The open attitude of full acceptance of the subtle energies (the DEEP elements as we call them) is crucial in releasing them. This is the direct and very simple way of overcoming all the automatic repression, stopping, discarding or 'explaining' of these energies – and instead to simply perceive them for what they are and allow them to complete their cycles of action as subtle energies and to flow out.

When introspecting in mind, heart and body, the person should not look for quick answers but spend the time necessary to let new, firsthand observations form. As in all forms of DEEP Clearing, a receptive and non-judgmental attitude of witnessing and receptively confronting of the case phenomena is crucial for success (see The Clearer's Professional Conduct). The instruction to the client "Assume your Mindful Self" (or a Higher Self, etc.) can be useful if the client gets too involved and starts dramatizing and *"being"* the Aspects and phenomena or gets caught up in long rational explanations rather than witnessing and confronting the phenomena *as* Aspects (separate entities) of self. The whole exercise is to take off any stops of the aspects and allow them to freely express themselves in the session. Their energies will release if we simply freely accept them. And this, as mentioned above, corresponds very well to Releasing (Lester Levinson) where the main steps are to perceive negative emotions and freely accept them. By experiencing and accepting them fully they complete their cycles as stored energies in our system and simply fizzle out.

Chapter 2
Deep Awareness and Aspect Clearing Procedure Explained

(Sept 17, 2018, updated March 19, 2020)

Definitions:

Deep Awareness: (1) It is about "how you feel inside" when you think of a certain problem.

(2) It could be called the *body awareness* of an issue or situation. It consists of all the subtle phenomena and things that are going on in the body and energy body, rather than in the mind.

(3) A feeling or energy in your body connected to a certain situation or issue. When a person sits quietly while concentrating on the issue, he/she can find these energies in or around the body. It can be in the form of emotions, feelings, body-sensations, pictures, tensions, masses, shapes, flows, etc. It may take a minute or so to develop and fully reveal itself. This is because we are contacting material we have totally forgotten about. We may possibly have denied and suppressed it. In DAC we bring it out, accept it and release it piece by piece, item by item.

The Deep Awareness is the raw material of Aspects.

Aspect: (1) The part of us that holds the negative reaction.

(2) The state and condition of the energy body in response to a certain issue. It can be seen as a stuck identity consisting of subtle energies and behavioral patterns.

(3) A part of us or sub-personality that seems to have a life of its own. It exists below the consciousness level. An Aspect may express itself as irrational emotional reactions, such as fear, anxiety or anger not called for; also as feelings and body-sensations hard to describe, masses and tensions. Aspects are typically formed in moments of puzzlement, upset or overwhelm. In hindsight you find them by looking for stuck moments related to the issue. If you think of an upsetting situation and look inside in your body, you will sense all these tensions and feelings connected to the situation. (See also Deep Awareness).

Item: (1) It is the descriptive name or label we put on an Aspect.

(2) A *representation* of how the energy body feels, behaves and reacts regarding a certain issue.

(3) This is *the name, description or symbol* we give an Aspect. The Item can be a mental picture of ourselves in a certain situation; it can be a more abstract shape, picture or symbol; or it can be a mental shape or picture of a person we dealt with. It can also simply be an energy or mass in the body, such as a nervous stomach or a stiff neck.

The DAC Steps with Comments

Deep Awareness Step (Aware step - AW)

AW: "Can you find a Deep Awareness connected to the issue?" (Look for juicy Aspect.)

"How does it feel in the body?" Describe, including feelings, energies, etc. Capture it in words.

Re: Aware step. At first, the person sits quietly, looking into the body and energy body in order to become aware of these phenomena. Then the person begins to describe them in words. Usually they contain feelings, emotions, energies, pictures, thoughts, impulses etc. It may be connected to a certain event or scenery. The person keeps working on the description until it feels just right. By 'juicy Aspect' we mean it has some energy to it in the form of emotions, feelings, sensations, etc. With 'Body', let us repeat, we mean the whole bio-field, the energy field in and around the body.

Perception (Sense step - S)

Re: Sense step. The person is asked to examine the Deep Awareness phenomena from the outside and sense them. The person will find answers to some or all of the perception questions; the person then sums it up by giving a physical description – as the person sees it now. The phenomena and the state of the energy body become more real and tangible doing this exercise. Sometimes the step brings up hidden parts of the Aspect or the whole scene, such as the voice of a participant, the smell of the person's perfume, the noise of the place, etc. All this is something we welcome. Additional questions can be asked to make the potential Aspect into a 'thing' – something that can be sensed and perceived as being out there, separate from ourselves.

Each answer to a question below is taken up and discharged. The discharge mainly happens by close inspection until the person is fully satisfied with the answer. It usually makes little sense to repeat the question as we are establishing more 'objective' facts.

S: "Does what you perceive (the Deep Awareness) have:

1s. Location? This can be in or around the body. It can sometimes manifest itself in several locations as one phenomenon or unit, such as in the stomach and in the face at the same time.

2s. Form or shape? It can have a distinct geometrical shape or – more likely – an irregular form characterized by energetic activity.

3s. Texture? Is it dense, a ridge, more like a dispersal? Air, liquid or solid? Are there motion of flows inside? Anything like that are typical answers.

4s. Color? Makes the person take a closer look. Typical answers are white, grey, blue, transparent, or no color.

5s. Size? This may already have been established. Sometimes it helps isolate the extent of the phenomena.

6s. Weight? Surprisingly, some of these items appear to have a considerable weight. Take whatever the person gives you.

7s. Touch or pressure (tactile)? If the phenomena press against body parts and organs it is usually clearly sensed as pressure. Again, many of the questions may already have been answered. If so, simply move on quickly. Yet several of the questions will get the person take an extra look or 'sense action' and get a better grip on the character and extent of the phenomena.

8s. Smell? 9s. Taste? Some items have a distinct smell or taste to them. This can be flattened by repeating.

10s. Sound? Sometimes there is sound connected to an item. It is not common, but it can be important to catch when present.

11s. Temperature? Some items are distinctly hot or cold. The person will usually perceive items at normal body temperature as not having a temperature. But we are interested in if items appear hot (over body temperature) or cold (below body temperature). Take whatever answer the person gives.

12s. Body-sensation? Here we are at the borderline of normal DEEP questions. We have included it here as it often brings out the description we use to friends and family – not to mention in the doctor's office.

Finding the Item that represents the Aspect/Deep Awareness. (What are you?) (Item)

Item: "What can we call this?"

Re: Item step. We need a label for the Aspect. (Sometimes we have gotten one already and only need to confirm it or finalize it). The person tries out different answers. Both the person and Aspect will feel good about it when the right representation has been found. It's an 'ah ha moment' – body and mind will relax. Also remember:

Item: (2) A *representation* of how the energy body feels, behaves and reacts regarding a certain issue.
(3) This is *the name, description or symbol* we give an Aspect. The Aspect itself can be a mental picture of ourselves in a certain situation; it can be a more abstract shape, picture or symbol; or it can be a mental shape or picture of a person we dealt with. It can also simply be an energy or mass in the body, such as a nervous stomach or a stiff neck.
The act of naming things in itself is reassuring and therapeutic. You are applying the rational mind in identifying the problem; the part is brought into the awareness with some sort of clarity and a handle. It also helps the person to see it as a separate part and temporary condition that is not inherently part of the core personality.

Dialogue Step (Hello/OK – H/OK)

This step helps separate out the Aspect from self. The Aspect is typically an ignored and suppressed part that we have excelled in not listening to. It is built around stopped impulses and all the stuck emotions and feelings that they can assemble. The Dialogue step helps loosen up the situation by allowing it all to be expressed, acknowledged and accepted. All the piled up energy in these hidden, forgotten and suppressed communications is suddenly revealed and allowed to complete their cycles of action.

We use the well-known DEEP tool of Hello-OK. First we do a few rounds of Hello-OK between person and Aspect. This establishes a communication line along which the messages can travel. H/OK is run this way:

As (your name), say Hello to (Aspect).	As (your name), is there s/t you want to say to (Aspect)?
As (Aspect), receive that communication.	As (Aspect) receive that.
As (Aspect), say Hello to (your name).	As (Aspect), is there s/t you want to say to (your name)?
As (your name) receive that communication.	As (your name), receive that, etc.

We use the forms "As (your name)" and "As (Aspect)" in order to put some distance between the items and the spiritual Being. Both the personality (the client's ID) and the Aspect are creations of the Being – but not the actual Being itself. The formulation helps the Being take ownership and control of both sides.

DEEP Step (DEEP – D)

We are now fully ready for the DEEP step where we release and integrate any additional stuck energies. We find the thoughts and intentions that are at the core of a DEEP package. We have since first edition of DAC added a whole series of Thought questions as these can be very productive. It is a series of questions that at first glance may seem self-repeating or a hit and miss – and maybe they are. Still, we get some important 'hits' that can have long-reaching consequences and positive effects. *Also, if ,say, the Feeling question brings out 5 answers we note all 5 answers down and take each up in turn and make sure all feelings are released.*

As a difference from the description in the original DEEP Clearing book, we focus on one answer (such as an identified Feeling) and release that as much as we can. It may uncover an underlying feeling which is taken up before we are done with that item. We do not automatically ask for thoughts and efforts. The feeling may simply release rather quickly and that is that. The many questions will catch them anyway. Also, we are now more interested in body-sensations than the Efforts. The Effort band is the body band. And the dominant content is body-sensations and body-language in most persons and situations.

If a Feeling runs long it does however make sense to ask if there is a message or wording coming out of that item. We can then run the Thought and then the Feeling as 1, 2. 1, 2.

1.) "Feel that 'annoyance' (feeling) as deeply as you can". 2.) "Say the thought, 'This isn't fair". You can also add a 3rd leg and ask into body-language like, "Can you show the body-language present", and the person may clench his fists and tense up the body to demonstrate. But adding a 2nd and 3rd leg is only called for if the original item runs long and slow.

So the instructions are*: **what you use as additional tools to release a feeling or another DEEP item is now up to the clearer's judgment.*** Don't insist on that there is an Effort, that there is a Thought that can be expressed or the like. In theory there is, but not always in practice; or it may contain minimal charge and better be left alone. Instead, the situation taken up can contain 5 different emotions that each should be run and released individually.

Note: The person may originate additional items during the run and it can be difficult to determine what is still charged and alive. Although we prefer to run one item cleanly to its release and flat point, we have sometimes used to make a short list and run them 1, 2, 3, 4, 5,- 1, 2, 3, 4, 5, etc. You instruct the person to report if one goes flat. Then you run the remaining in sequence, say: 1, 3, 4, 5 as 2 went flat. At some point they are all handled. The items were simply so interwoven and running them this way takes care of whatever is there.

Getting the energy off an item

Since the publishing of the basic book, it has also become clear that what we are after is the pure energy in a DEEP item. Getting caught up in the incident and circumstances can work as a distraction. This does not change our basic technique of Repeat and Tell but we now see it more clearly as two separate actions, each with a distinct function.

The Repeat part gets the underlying energy and we direct the person to get its vibration, frequency; taste it so to speak. The person should accept it as energy and let it flow its natural course as that completes its cycle.

In the Tell part we let the person tell freely what pops up – sometimes at some length. This takes care of similar experiences and incidents in a fast and easy way. So we even invite that. But we always direct the person back to identify the pure energy of the item in question. "Get the energy of that emotion and allow it to flow", "get the energy in your body of that statement – feel that energy deeply" , "Get the energy and vibration of that energy and allow it to be present", and the like are very effective directions after the Tell part. Sometimes the spotting of the pure energy takes all the pressure off the item like a letting the air out of a balloon. So there is a distinct difference between reliving the story and the pure charge, the pure energy that makes it troublesome.

Yet identifying the story line has its own value. It takes care of a whole bunch of similar incidents and we learn from reviewing exactly what happened and see all the contexts. We evaluate what happened; we often compare it to present life and circumstances – and that is how we transform trauma and stress to life-experience. Accomplishing that is the hallmark of DEEP.

Thoughts, Decisions

When it comes to running thoughts and decisions we start out with an answer from a Thought question; sometimes we simply pick up a statement the person uttered during the running. We take the statement and first we run it plainly, instructing the person to say it once as he really means it and then await an acknowledgement before he says it again. When this has run its course, the clearer asks the person to say it in different moods. The clearer may pick likely moods from the emotional scale, starting with likely low moods. Usually a statement gives meaning in some moods but not all. The trick is to see a scenario where it does make sense to say it in the mood picked. What often happens is that we hit a tone that really draws 'blood' – or at least charge. The same statement can be charged in several moods. An explanation could be that the thought has been used in many situations as a thought from one's basic arsenal. In other words the statement discharges when we hit these moods and this discharge is a valuable bonus. We start low and work our way up the moods – often ending up in humor.

Also, especially when it comes to command phrases or Dictates (statements adopted from other people in a traumatic incident) it is of great value to identify the likely source of the Dictate and have the person say it from that viewpoint, "As your father, say 'you must do your homework – or else...!'" could be an example.

The DAC DEEP Questions

In DAC we use the series of questions listed below There may be more than one DEEP element or item on each question. Each item is taken up separately and released. Each question is then repeated as needed and taken to 'no more response'. Whatever DEEP element pops up is flattened, also those that are not logical answers to what is asked. It has popped up and presented itself so you simply run it and ask the question again. The questions are simply a system to find 'something to run'. What pops up is the real deal.

D: "Are there any: 1d. Emotions? 2d. Feelings? 3d. Body sensations? 4d. Pains? 5d. Body language or Posture? 6d. Actions or reactions? 7d. Mental efforts? 8d. Held back efforts? 9d. Hide reaction? 10d. Freeze reaction? 11d. Flight reaction? 12d. Fight reaction? 13d. Masses or flows?

Additional 'Thought' questions.

Anything reactive that pops up is flattened, as long as it qualifies as a DEEP element. The clearer may pick and choose from the list. You should name the issue rather than calling it 'that issue'.

Q1: is there a good reason why you have (that item/issue)?
Q2: is there s/t in you that makes it an issue?
Q3: is there a reactive thought that is part of (that issue)?
Q4: is there some way it is good for you to have (the issue)?,
Q5: do you somehow gain from having (the issue)?
Q6: is there somehow a way (the issue) serves you?
Q7: does the (issue) in some way help you?
Q8: is there s/t you would you lose, if you didn't have (that issue)?
Q9: if the mind would find a reason why it is good for you to have... (issue) – what would it be?
Q10: is there a decision about "it must not happen again" built into this issue?
Q11: is there a warning signal built into this issue?
Q12: is (issue) a solution that appears as a solution or way out from s/t else?

Two Sides

Ideally we do the DEEP steps on both the Aspect and client's ID. We ask for the side the person is most interested in and begin there. Both the personality (the client's ID) and the Aspect are creations of the Being – but not the actual Being itself.

If any of the above DEEP questions gets a significant reaction, run it DEEP style right away using repeated mindful perception (Repeat and Tell) and other applicable tools. The person has to accept and allow the energy to be there – to let go of any suppressors and repressors and 'taste' the pure energy. That is what allows the energy to release and discharge. Again, the questions comprise a system. What pops up from the subconscious energy systems is the real deal. Make full use of the DEEP tools when you have found a 'real deal item' to run.

Chapter 3
DAC - Additional Data

(Sep 9, 2018, updated March 19, 2020.)

Finding the Juicy Aspects

When running Deep Awareness and Aspect Clearing it is important to know that each Aspect is different. Each Aspect, it appears, has a life of its own. Most of them are sensitive parts of ourselves that have been denied and repressed – or simply left behind. They need to be handled with respect and genuine interest. Now is the time to listen to them; listen to their grievances, messages, warnings and intentions that won't go away. It is not enough to just brush them off.

The items and the process may to some seem to be slow going but one should spend the time needed on each step. Basically, on the initial steps we are (1) finding a potential Aspect (Deep Awareness step); (2) perceiving it as an object and phenomena separate from ourselves (Perception step); (3) and then seeking an answer to the question, *"What are you?" or "What would represent the Deep Awareness?"* (Item step).

We are not satisfied with quick and glib answers. You know, if you socially ask someone, 'How are you today?' you usually get, 'I am fine', and you didn't learn anything. If you ask a person, 'What are you?' you will get a title or profession and not the feel or energy of the person. The answers we want should have some 'body' to them; some mass, emotion and sensation. So ask into that rather than using pat questions. Invite the person to pause and sense what comes. That is what the DEEP Awareness and the Perception steps are about. We are looking for the potential energies that affect our behavior, health and way of thinking negatively when left on automatic. They get triggered by life – and Bam!

The Deep Awareness Step ('Aware')

The cue card question on the Deep Awareness step is:
"Can you find a Deep Awareness connected to [the issue at hand]?"
"How does it feel in the body?" Describe, including feelings, etc. Capture it in words.

We first have to spend the time necessary to find the Deep Awareness that has some impact. You apply Deep Awareness and look into your body – mainly chest and heart region. But other areas can attract attention, especially belly and abdomen. The throat and physical head (as different from mind) are sometimes in play. **Something will attract your attention and that is where you go.** You look for something to form. The first step is to find the energy that turns on when contemplating the issue. Don't just settle for an instant pop-up, like a picture, title, or name. The pop-up may just be a little flag marking that something is there. Sometimes the person will just repeat old complaints. Just running the surface items or old complaints is an old mistake from other methods.

Try to look behind what popped up. We should find something that seems to have some mass to it; something that is capable of influencing our behavior. It should turn on some kind of body sensation or feeling. Usually it will feel familiar and related to situations from your life. *Put some words on exactly how the item appears and feels. An accurate verbal description that seems to 'click' is what we want.*

If you find nothing behind the pop-up, Fine! You take the pop-up of course and run that. It may have presented itself readily and that's it. But as a rule, if a client doesn't seem to find the juicy version of the potential Aspect you should ask him to look around to find it. You can ask him to scan the body with his attention and take a thorough look inside; or you can ask him if there is a juicy mass connected to the pop-up answer – an area that has feelings, sensations and mass connected to it – a Deep Awareness and potential Aspect that has impact and command value.

The Perception Step ('Sense')

The cue card questions are:

S: "Does what you perceive (the Deep Awareness) have: 1s. Location? 2s. Form or shape? 3s. Texture? 4s. Color? 5s. Size? 6s. Weight? 7s. Touch or pressure (tactile)? 8s. Smell? 9s. Taste? 10s. Sound? 11s. Temperature? 12. Body-sensation?

The step helps sensing and seeing the potential Aspect as separate from ourselves.

We use our senses all the time. We use them to navigate in the physical world. We use sounds, sights, smells, tastes, touch – and an array of finer perceptions that we pick up without using the body directly. All these senses are used to understand and navigate in the external world.

On the Perception step we direct our senses towards the potential Aspect. We usually think of the Aspect as 'the way we are'; the Perception step helps sensing and seeing it as a separate unit or entity. We direct the essential senses at the Aspects and their world and then sum up what we 'see'.

(Note: This step is a 'non-DEEP' step. Usually, the elements we are most interested in in DEEP are thoughts, emotions, feelings, sensations and efforts. These energies make up and determine our thinking, emotional life and behavior – our subjective experience of life, an internal experience. On the Sense step, we want to perceive the phenomena more objectively, an external experience.)

The Item Step ('Item')

The cue card version is:

Find the Item that represents the Aspect or Deep Awareness. (What are you?)

"What can we call this?"

By now we have a pretty good idea and feel of the potential Aspect. It is time to name it. We have to find a name or label or symbolic picture, *a representation,* that makes it possible to talk about it and handle it in a more concrete way. As an example we could find 'Sleeping Beauty' (from Grimm's fairytales) as Item.

Again, it may take a little work. Try out different labels and symbolic pictures and compare them to the Deep Awareness. If the dominating trait is an emotional situation from your life, you can imagine yourself in such a situation; 'a sad me at the dinner table, 10 years old'; 'a horrified me in the accident, age 17', etc. But, as explained elsewhere, it can be just about anything. At some point it will 'click'. It feels just right. The client will relax in body and mind and have an 'Ah ha moment'. You have found it. You as the clearer are ready to go on to the next step.

The Dialogue Step

The Dialogue Step is just that: the Aspect has something to say and you listen and acknowledge. You start out with saying Hello and receiving a hello back and acknowledge. After a few rounds of this there is established a communication line. Then you go into a dialogue. You go back and forth telling whatever comes to mind until the conversation is completed Take your time, and as long as interchange and changes occur you keep it up doing the step. You keep it up until both parties have no more to say.

Dialogue Step (Hello/OK – H/OK)

We use the tool of Hello-OK: First a few rounds of Hello-OK between person and Aspect. H/OK is run this way:

As (your name), say Hello to (Aspect).	As (your name), is there s/t you want to say to (Aspect)?
As (Aspect), receive that communication.	As (Aspect) receive that.
As (Aspect), say Hello to (your name).	As (Aspect), is there s/t you want to say to (your name)?
As (your name) receive that communication.	As (your name), receive that, etc.

We use the forms "As (your name)" and "As (Aspect)" in order to put some distance between the items and the spiritual Being. Both the personality (the client's ID) and the Aspect are creations of the Being – but not the actual Being itself. The formulation helps the Being take ownership and control of both sides.

Communication and Discharge

The communication factor should always be present in a DAC session – whether you are with a client or doing it solo. The basic steps in communication are: Cause-*Distance*-Effect or Sender-*Distance*-Receiver. Somebody speaks (sends), reaches over a distance to another who listens (receives). These steps go both ways in live, successful communications. So when you communicate with an Aspect you are actually creating this vital distance. You are creating the space and separation necessary for a communication to take place. Initially with Aspects there was no Distance. Cause and Effect were not separated but occurred simultaneously. There was a collapse of Cause and Effect. This collapse forms a trigger, a short circuit, and an automatic push-button mechanism.

Using the procedure, you allow yourself to be cause and then effect – to talk to and to listen to the Aspect; to send and then receive. There is a separation that allows an exchange of energies and information. You see the Aspect as an entity being out there and realize it isn't natively a part of you. The short circuit is taken apart. Any frozen energy and information contained in the Aspect and the situation is allowed to flow both ways and thus an orderly discharge takes place until it has completed its cycle.

The important point as a Clearer in doing any of the steps is to be observant and keep working on the steps that are moving things around. This means that communication and discharge are occurring. You will *on the one hand* learn which steps to emphasize with a certain client or type of

Aspect. And, *on the other hand*, you will also learn to do the steps lightly that do little for the client or possibly skip the step altogether.

Still, the communication factor between client and item at hand is the essence of this method – as it is in any clearing procedure, whether our own DEEP Clearing or any other form of self-improvement. Discharging anything in therapy, it could be said, consists of separating Cause from Effect and completing these old communications, whether they were frozen, repressed, suppressed or totally hidden away in the body or subconscious mind; whether they consisted of information, perceptions, emotions, sensations, feelings, thoughts, or physical tensions and forces. We find them, thaw them up with our awareness and unbiased curiosity and let them flow to their natural release and we are done. This is accomplished by the free exchange of information and energies – primarily from the Aspect to the person but in response to relevant questions and good acknowledgements that signal that the Aspect's situation, messages and energies have been received and understood.

Keeping this in mind, you will understand, that what techniques to use and emphasize may change over time. Typically we use all steps thoroughly early on and as time goes by we may end up with a very abbreviated version of DAC where only the beginning steps are needed.

The 'Deep Awareness' through the Dialogue steps, while the communication factor is prominently present, is sometimes all it takes with an experienced client. The person tends to get the experience of the DEEP step right there and then and discharge the Aspect completely.

Notes on the DEEP Step

On this the DEEP step we may see all kinds of behaviors and bodily experiences, feelings, emotions and thoughts unfold. It is addressing subjective experience, the hallmark of the DEEP techniques. Here again, it is important to be in good, empathic contact with the Aspect. Once more, the communication factor is the active ingredient.

In the modality called Focusing (and in several other modalities) they use what is called Emphatic or Active Listening. They repeat back what the client (or Aspect) says, maybe in an implicit or paraphrased form, showing that they have understood it. We find, that using this form of communication throughout too often leads to misunderstandings and evaluations. It takes a master to use this technique without fallouts.

So we use really paying attention to the person and acknowledging what they say and occasionally "I understand and accept you have [a feeling of fear]" or the like. Use whatever seems to work with the client but don't repeat it all like a parrot. In my book that can be quite tedious and sometimes upsetting to the client.

In regard to body-experience and behavior; feelings, emotions; and thoughts, the principal DEEP energies – we have given a wording in the cue card version that seems to work most of the time. But this is not to say that in a specific situation it is not important to observe the DEEP phenomena that really are going on and ask into them in a relevant and intelligent way and receive, understand and acknowledge the messages, energies and phenomena you get.

Notes on Emotions and Feelings

When we go into **Emotions and Feelings** we are asking for a base vibration you could say. Sometimes we call it State of Mind or Vibration. However, sometimes we get a torrent of conflicting emotions, such as fear, apathy, surprise, anger, triumph. It could reflect a whole action cycle from being attacked to successfully fighting the attacker off. Each emotion contains a basic action pattern or strategy and what happens when a real person has all these conflicting emotions, is that the different strategies are considered – if only briefly. They are simply flashing by. In DEEP we take each item in turn and run it out.

The DEEP step may sometimes trigger a known or emerging incident. It is legitimate to simply run the incident, going through it several times. You can use formal DEEP Incident Clearing, for that matter. But in DAC we don't ask for incidents up front as it all too often has led to that the client feels pressed to come up with, or invent, a scenario that could fit. We want to avoid that. The Aspects are typically complex 'creatures' or entities that are composed of many situations and events and the client's reactions and considerations on top of that. To try to sort out each Aspect's history of creation can be as difficult as solving the murder mystery of a peasant who was murdered in 1153 A.D. The solid evidence is just long lost and missing. We use the tactic of Alexander the Great, when he was confronted with the Gordian Knot. He swung his sword and cut the hopelessly entangled knot over. Voila! The mystery was solved.

Dictate/Intention/Thought

Here we are really looking for what is holding the Aspect together. There may be various thoughts and stories that surface and this is all fine. But what we are after is the core thoughts, dictates and intentions. Among these there is a central purpose or goal the Aspect is operating on or displaying. *The whole package **dictates** something.* It could be seen as the basic message the Aspect has been unable to deliver. There may be a number of thoughts that form the Aspect. So we simply take this apart in a systematic way. But in the final analysis it comes down to one central message, the dictate or intention that dominates and motivates the Aspect. It can be simple dictates like 'Get out of there', 'To please the other person', 'To isolate self', 'To dominate', 'To avoid something', 'To keep up a façade', etc. In practice we just work our way down the list of thought questions. This, that and the other thought will pop up from the subconscious. We handle and release each thought as it reveals itself. We just start at the beginning and go forward. Finding a good wording that expresses an intent or message may take a little work as it was never put into words. But the task at hand is to find a simple wording that captures the intent or dictate. You allow the person to keep working at it and change the wording as he sees fit. This action of putting the unknown and vague thought or intent into words is very therapeutic in itself. It suddenly stands out and can be separated from self. We can now receive and release the message or intent.

You can of course also find conflicting intentions, either of your own making or the Aspect's own intent being opposed by another, a Polarity. You can find two Aspects in conflict and run the one after the other. Or you can go back and forth between the two intentions, sensing one after the other, and flatten the Polarity that way.

As we go along this way, just following the list of thought questions, we will often find that there is a central thought or intention. This is where it all started. It is like the speck of sand that formed the pearl in the oyster. The feelings, emotions and impulses are outer layers or attachments to that. All the other thoughts found somehow attached to or modified that central intent. It's really the complexities of experiences, oppositions, own repressions, second thoughts, and all the emotional upheavals that make the package into a complex mystery. And mysteries like that are really 'unfinished business' that keep attracting attention, ponderings and wonderings. "What is this?" What really happened?", "Was it my fault?" "What should I have done instead?" "Who was really to blame?"

But once you find the central intention you have found "Who has done it?" like in murder mysteries. You have gotten to the bottom of the heap, to the center of the pearl. And you have found the initial speck, the basic intention. We believe this is what Dr. Gerbode talks about when he defines Charge. He defines it something like: Charge is repressed, unfulfilled intention and attention. To get to the Intention we first have to do a lot of digging. All the confusion, the overwhelm, the conflicting vectors, the stories and smaller intentions, the stuck attentions, emotions, and impulses – all the colliding frequencies we find around it have to be removed bit by bit. All that is what ties up and traps the intention and attention. It freezes or represses the original intent – while keeping attracting attention as it is an unsolved mystery.

Completing Aspects

The overall purpose of doing all these steps is of course to completely discharge irrational or counter-productive Aspects, one at a time. Once that is accomplished for the Aspect we are working on, we are done with that action. This can happen very quickly – or sometimes it hasn't happened even when we have done all the steps on the Aspect. First, here are some important definitions:

Overall Endpoint*:* It is important to understand that there is what we call an **Endpoint** that we go for. It is the point in the session where the Aspect is resolved and fully discharged. The Aspect will either integrate or it will blow off. Once that is obtained, we have gotten what we were after and the procedure is ended. We can start on a new Aspect or simply end the session.

Step Endpoint: Likewise, each step of the procedure can reach *its own Endpoint* before we have gotten to the end of the step. Typically, it stops generating 'electricity' when contacted. The person cannot get a response anymore; it is hard to keep up interest as 'nothing more is going on' with the technique. The step has simply gone flat. If so, recognize the fact and move on to the next step.

No Discharge: This is not the same as saying, if the person cannot contact anything to begin with 'it must already be flat'. This situation could simply mean that another technique should be used. Material and discharge are not always available, even with highly sensitive material. *It comes down to the communication factor.* Can the person contact the material in the first place? If not, no discharge will occur. To the Clearer this means that he/she will have to do something else. Repair the communication factor (see below) or simply use another technique entirely, such as DEEP Incident Clearing or DEEP Subject Clearing.

Unflat Step: *You should also recognize that some steps need to be continued or repeated in order to flatten completely.* If it is still 'alive', when you are done with the formal points in a step, you should do some more work before moving on. Sometimes that consists of repeating the step; sometimes you simply extend it by doing similar actions; and sometimes you may use DEEP tools – special techniques that are found in the DEEP book. The latter would be used by a professional for efficiency but may not be strictly needed in solo.

Repairing the Communication Factor: Before deciding that 'DAC is too difficult' or the like, the communication factor should be reviewed. This would include making sure the client uses most of the time to introspect (looking into the energy-body or biofield) and not just being talkative or social with the Clearer. The Clearer is just the rope holder while the client reports 'from the depth of the cave'. The client may also have preconceived ideas and invalidate what he/she observes and finds. "This is nonsense", "this isn't possible", "this is silly", "there is nothing in there" etc. Such biases can be taken up and discussed and possibly run as suppressors or counter-intentions. We have used DEEP Body Clearing to help persons get in better contact with their bodies and the Deep Awarenesses. In some cases we have recommended Mindfulness meditation as a good preparation to doing DAC. Also, persons who have done a lot of body-work seem in general to be more ready for DAC and DEEP in general.

The Clearer should also review his/her approach. Is he willing to accept the client's answers without bias or judgment? Does he acknowledge the answers appropriately? Can he understand and handle apparent detours and pop up statements? Can he follow the client without back off? This is covered fully in the DEEP book as Communication Exercises.

To summarize, if a step seems hard to complete, *the first thing to review is the communication factors.* Make sure the client is receptive, unbiased and curious about what comes from the Aspect. Being a good receiver or listener who deals with and acknowledges appropriately whatever comes up, goes for both client and Clearer.

If the Procedure Runs Long

If the overall Endpoint hasn't happened when we have done the whole procedure there are some actions that can be taken.

We can simply start the whole procedure from the top. Especially reviewing what name we called the Aspect and exactly where it is located in or around the body is important. It should be suspected that there are errors. So do it carefully in a fresh unit of time. Confirm or correct the wording of the Item and its location. Also make sure you haven't overlooked the real Item, the mass and the feelings part. Sometimes you have only gotten hold of the surface, the little flag sticking up, and the real juicy item is still in place. The flag can be an attached entity that is echoing one's own Aspect.

Another source of puzzlement, that is not uncommon, is that there is another Aspect connected closely to the same issue. Major issues, like bad relationships, fear of speaking in public, anger bursts, irrational fears, etc. can be riddled with a number of Aspects that need to be addressed individually. Check if the original Aspect has been handled, and if 'Yes', look for another Aspect related to the issue.

If you have done a considerable amount of session work and things have become murky or massy, the best move may be to call it a day and possibly wait a couple of days until it all has calmed down and settled. Then give it a fresh start – not necessarily trying to sort out possible past mistakes. Just give it a fresh start, looking at what is available now in present time.

Mindful Contemplation – The Shower Technique

We humans are complex Beings. That goes for our bodies, our minds and our relationships. Even after very successful sessions a person can feel somewhat electrically charged or energized, though now in a pleasant way – like after a good massage. There seems to be echoes of what has just been run that still resonate in mind and body. In DAC we use a simple technique that ensures the full benefits from this reverberation. Masses and energies have been moved around during the session and a discharge has taken place. A new equilibrium of forces needs to be established.

Sit quietly by yourself and focus on the area of body and mind that was just addressed in the session. Quiet your thoughts and just perceive the area in play. Perceive it as energy without trying to speculate about what is going on. You are simply creating a quiet space, time and atmosphere internally. Now flow appreciation, admiration and even love into the area without necessarily adding any thoughts or significance to the flow. This contemplation and appreciation will facilitate further discharge and allow more energies and masses to run off you, so to speak, or find their place in a new and lighter balance. *This action is like taking a shower after a good workout – and that's why we call it the Shower Technique.* The action can increase the benefits from the session with up to 20%.

Good Hunting

The above are the basic instructions, the tips and advice that go with the procedure. Deep Awareness and Aspect Clearing can be done in a formal session setting, with a practitioner and client, or it can be done solo. Solo works best after the person has gone through a series of guided sessions. The person may still need or want guided sessions later, if difficult issues arise.

Solo DAC: When doing DAC solo it's a good idea to keep a log. Write down what step you are working on and the essential answers you get. Also experiment with writing out detailed answers. Putting a rather intangible phenomenon in writing is sometimes very useful. You see it on the paper now. Use the worksheets to draw the Aspects – just simple sketches that maybe only make sense to you. If you are an artist, have at it!

Keeping such a step-by-step log helps with the concentration and self-discipline – something that is highly needed when you are on your own. A thing that makes the technique well suited for solo work, compared to most other techniques, is the detailed step-by-step procedure and the various perception exercises. With DAC you are really giving your biofield (the electro-magnetic energy body), your mind and physical body a workover. Your life will change for the better. You will discover many amazing and surprising things about what makes you tick – and what didn't make you tick for that matter. The beauty of it is that negative points and shortcomings, all the old dirt and dead bugs in the clockwork, can be taken care of and you will experience some high moments of relief and happiness.

In the Scientology system there is a state of existence, called Clear. According to the definition of this ideal state, a Clear is at cause over mental matter, energy, space and time in his/her own world. A Clear is fully in command of his/her own mind in other words. The Clear person can think rationally and analytically under the most trying circumstances. Obviously that is a desirable state of being. You can easily see how Deep Awareness and Aspect Clearing goes towards a similar goal. In DAC we keep locating subtle energies and mental phenomena consisting of mental matter, energy, space and time. We are doing exercises with them and integrating them. In other words, we gain a high level of control over what we call the Repressed Mind – the part of our subconscious that plays tricks on us.

In Deep Awareness and Aspect Clearing you will however experience a catharsis of your emotional life as well. You will experience emotional healing. It is not all about being rational and analytical. You will clear up your emotional life and include your emotions and intuitions as important guiding systems and valued life qualities.

You will integrate and align many sub-identities, the Aspects, with your core-being. Other Aspects will simply disappear or blow. You become whole again. This is integrity – being one's own authentic self even under trying circumstances. When doing Aspect Clearing, you will experience many highpoints where your whole being is flooded with joy and fresh vitality – with new inspiration. And that is really what we are aiming at in Deep Awareness and Aspect Clearing.

That is what we want for you.

We wish you Good Hunting!

Rolf Dane, Ability One Group.
September 9, 2018.
Revised March 19, 2020.

Definitions for Deep Awareness and Aspect Clearing

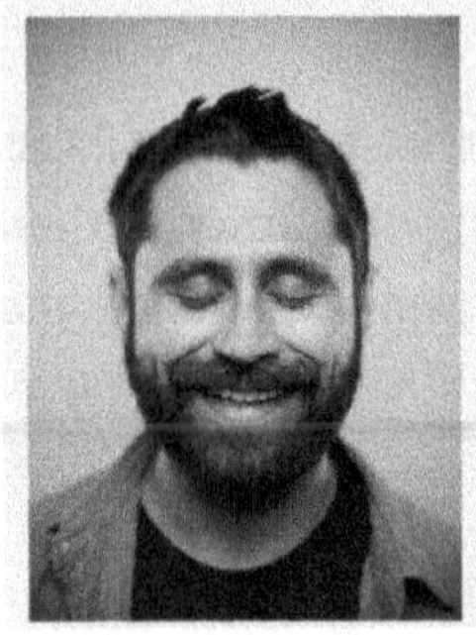  ***"You look into your body and sense how it feels inside. It may take a minute or so to really get in touch with what is there."***	**Deep Awareness:** (1) It is about *"how you feel inside"* when you think of a certain problem. (2) It could be called the *body awareness* of an issue or situation. It consists of all the subtle things that are going on in the body and energy body, rather than in the mind. (3) A feeling or energy in your body connected to a certain situation or issue. When a person sits quietly while concentrating on the issue, he/she can find these energies in or around the body. It can be in the form of emotions, feelings, pictures, tensions, impulses, masses, shapes, flows, etc. It may take a minute or so to develop and fully reveal itself. This is because we are contacting material we have totally forgotten about. We may have denied, suppressed and fought it. Simply allowing it to flow and accept it releases this charge; It completes its cycle of action when allowed to do so. *The Deep Awareness is the raw material of Aspects.*
 ***"You describe in words what you find. You are looking at a strange world of feelings and perceptions. 'Is it fantasy?' 'Am I just making it up?' you may ask. But No! It's your inner world that desperately wants to speak to you."***	**Aspect:** (1) The part of us that holds the negative reaction. (2) The state and condition of the energy body in response to a certain issue. It can be seen as a stuck identity consisting of subtle energies and behavioral patterns. (3) A part of us or a sub-personality that seems to have a life of its own. It exists below the consciousness level. An Aspect may express itself as irrational emotional impulses and reactions, including fear, anxiety or anger not called for; also as feelings hard to describe, masses and tensions. **Aspects are typically formed in moments of puzzlement, upset or overwhelm**. In hindsight *you find them by looking for stuck moments related to the issue.* If you think of an upsetting situation and look inside in your body, you will sense all these tensions, impulses, body-sensations and feelings connected to the situation. (See also Deep Awareness).

<table>
<tr>
<td>

Item: something personal,
sometimes weird. But it
represents the Aspect and
how it feels to the person.

"Here is the fun part: You express it as a symbol or 'thing'. Now you can move it around; you can speak with it. Soon you will become friends. It wasn't that bad after all."
</td>
<td>
Item: (1) It is the descriptive name or label we put on an Aspect.

(2) A representation of how the energy body feels, behaves and reacts regarding a certain issue.

(3) This is the name, description or symbol we give an Aspect. The Item can be a mental picture of ourselves in a certain situation; it can be a more abstract shape, picture or symbol; or it can be a mental shape or picture of a person we dealt with. It can also simply be an energy or mass in the body, such as a nervous stomach or a stiff neck.
</td>
</tr>
</table>

Chapter 4
Some DAC Techniques

Repeat and Tell:

You have the person perceive and feel the DEEP element as deeply as possible. The person accepts the phenomena as an energy in the body-mind system; that is the Repeat part. The perception of the pure energy can discharge it very quickly as it appears to be a sort of static electricity.

The Tell part is to invite the person to tell whatever comes to mind in the form of thoughts, pictures, memories etc. This helps understand the context and integrate it as a learning – as life experience. "Sense it as deeply as you can – if something comes to mind, tell me about it", is the format. (From DEEP Toolbox.)

End points

There are various End points on techniques and actions. This is covered fully in DAC – Additional Data.

Three Times Solid (3xSolid)

You take a DEEP element or incident that is intangible or sometimes stuck and unmovable. You say "Make it more solid" 3 or more times; then "Hold it still" 3 or more times; then "Keep it from going away" 3 or more times. This routine makes the element more real and gives the person a sense of control over it. It can be used instead of Six Directions (see below) when the person seems unable to do the moving around of an item or incident.(From DEEP Character Clearing.)

Six Directions (6-D)

You take a DEEP element or incident that is intangible, stuck or 'unmovable' and put control in on it. "Place it above you"; "Place it below you"; "Place it to the right"; "Place it to the left"; "Place it in front of you"; "Place it to the back of you". In this way you move an item around that previously existed in the subconscious and exerted control over you. You simply take control instead of it taking control over you. (From Robert Ducharme's R3X.)

Dialogue or Hello/OK

A step in DAC. The routine can be used in many contexts – to handle polarities, unfinished business, old conflicts, etc. Whenever you see two poles, be it persons, groups or phenomena in opposition, consider using this technique. (Originally from Fritz Perls', Gestalt Therapy.)

Grounding a DEEP Item

1-Have the person connect the center of the body to the earth through the feet. Also have the person connect to the 'higher up' – be it to a higher self, a religious figure or God. Connected in this way, have the person sense the item in question. 2. The person can also 'shine a light into the energy, expand and dilute the energy. These are all ways of releasing the energy. The tools can be used one alone or in combination. (from Science of Releasing by Marc Rüedi.)

Fixed Ideas

In addition to Repeating and using different moods and viewpoints in handling thoughts and decisions, we have Fixed Ideas handling. 1. If a fixed idea won't release easily, try the following. Ask "To your mind, what is the opposite to Idea A?" (Answer: Idea B.) Then: "Get idea A. Get idea B" back and forth to unstick the thinking. 2. You can also use "How has idea A helped you? How has idea A harmed you?" back and forth. (From Heidrun Beer's DEEP manual.)

Before/After a Stuck Moment

"Recall a moment before the incident/stuck moment." " Recall a moment after the incident/stuck moment" can unstick shocks and the similar. (From Robert Ducharme's R3X.)

Deep Awareness and Aspect Clearing (DAC) – Prompt Sheet

The Clearer is running the session and is doing the necessary observations to control and tailor-make the use of DEEP tools as needed. We can address any issue known to self-improvement and therapy. We may use any suitable DEEP tool when something pops up.

Deep Awareness Step (Aware step - AW)

AW: "Can you find a Deep Awareness connected to the issue?" (Look for juicy Aspect.)
"How does it feel in the body?" Describe, including feelings, energies, etc. Capture it in words.

Re: Aware step. At first, the person sits quietly, looking into the body and energy body in order to become aware of these phenomena. Then the person begins to describe them in words – feelings, emotions, energies, pictures, thoughts, etc. It may be connected to a certain event or scenery. The person keeps working on the description until it feels just right.

Perception (Sense step - S)

Each answer to a question below is taken up and discharged. The discharge mainly happens by close inspection until the person is fully satisfied with the answer. It usually makes little sense to repeat the question as we are establishing more 'objective' facts.

S: "Does what you perceive (the Deep Awareness) have:
1s. Location?
2s. Form or shape?
3s. Texture?
4s. Color?
5s. Size?
6s. Weight?
7s. Touch or pressure (tactile)?
8s. Smell?
9s. Taste?
10s. Sound?
11s. Hot or cold? (Temperature)
12. Body-sensation?

Re: Sense step. The person is asked to examine the Deep Awareness phenomena from the outside and sense them. The person will find answers to some or all of the perception questions The phenomena and the state of the energy body become more real and tangible doing this exercise. Sometimes the step brings up hidden parts of the Aspect or a whole scene, such as the voice of a participant, the smell of the person's perfume, the noise of the place, etc. All this is something we welcome. Additional questions can be asked to make the potential Aspect into a 'thing' (an Aspect) – something that can be sensed and perceived as being out there, separate from ourselves.

<u>Finding the Item that represents the Aspect/Deep Awareness. (What are you?) (Item)</u>

Item: "What can we call this?"

Re: Item step. We need a label for the Aspect. (Sometimes we have gotten one already and only need to confirm it or finalize it). The person tries out different answers. Both the person and Aspect will feel good about it when the right representation has been found. It's an 'ah ha moment' – body and mind will relax.

<u>Dialogue Step (Hello/OK – H/OK)</u>

We use the tool of Hello-OK: First a few rounds of Hello-OK between person and Aspect. H/OK is run this way:

As (your name), say Hello to (Aspect).	As (your name), is there s/t you want to say to (Aspect)?
As (Aspect), receive that communication.	As (Aspect) receive that.
As (Aspect), say Hello to (your name).	As (Aspect), is there s/t you want to say to (your name)?
As (your name) receive that communication.	As (your name), receive that, etc.

We use the forms "As (your name)" and "As (Aspect)" in order to put some distance between the items and the spiritual Being. Both the personality (the client's ID) and the Aspect are creations of the Being – but not the actual Being itself. The formulation helps the Being take ownership and control of both sides.

<u>DEEP Step (DEEP – D)</u>

Then we do the DEEP step using whatever tools are necessary. We get into it by using below questions. There may be more than one DEEP element or item on each question. Each item is taken up separately and released. Each question is then repeated as needed and taken to 'no more answers'. Whatever DEEP element pops up is flattened, also those that are not logical answers to what is asked. It has popped up and presented itself so you simply run it and ask the question again. The questions are simply a system to find 'something to run'. What pops up is the real deal.

> ***D: Are there any: 1d. Emotions? 2d. Feelings? 3d. Body sensations? 4d. Pains? 5d. Body language or Posture? 12d Actions or reactions? Mental Efforts? Held back Efforts? 6d. Hide reaction? 7d. Asking for mercy or praying? 8d. Freeze reaction? 9d. Flight reaction? 10d. Fight reaction? 11d- Masses or flows? 12d Actions or reactions? 13d. Impulses?***

-- *** --

D: "Are there any:

- ***1d. Emotions?***
- ***2d. Feelings?***
- ***3d. Body sensations?***
- ***4d. Pains?***
- ***5d. Body language or Posture?***
- ***6d. Actions or reactions?***

7d. Mental efforts?
8d. Held back efforts?
9d. Hide reaction?
10d. Freeze reaction?
11d. Flight reaction?
12d. Fight reaction?
13d. Masses or flows?

Additional 'Thought' questions.

Anything reactive that pops up is flattened. as long as it qualifies as a DEEP element. The clearer may pick and choose from the list. You should name the issue rather than calling it 'that issue'.

Q1: is there a good reason why you have (that item/issue)?
Q2: is there s/t in yourself that makes it an issue?
Q3: is there a reactive thought that is part of (that issue)?
Q4: is there some way it is good for you to have (the issue)?,
Q5: do you somehow gain from having (the issue)?
Q6: is there somehow a way (the issue) serves you?
Q7: does the (issue) in some way help you?
Q8: is there s/t you would you lose, if you didn't have (that issue)?
Q9: if the mind would find a reason why it is good for you to have... (issue) – what would it be?
Q10: is there a decision about "it must not happen again" built into this issue?
Q11: is there a warning signal built into this issue?
Q12: is (issue) a solution that appears as a solution or way out from s/t else?

Two Sides: Ideally we do the DEEP step on both the Aspect and client's ID. We ask for the side the person is most interested in and begin there. If one of above questions gets a significant reaction, run it DEEP style right away using repeated mindful perception. Make full use of the DEEP tools as needed. Sometimes there is no 'other side' that can be found or having charge.

Chapter 5
How to Program DAC - Inspiration and Notes

It is not difficult to program DAC as you can follow the track of other programs and simply address the charge uncovered with DAC. For people who can run DAC well, it would simply be an extra DEEP technique that you use to handle emerging charge. It can go like this: you are running an ability-technique (see below) and a charged issue or situation emerges. You get the exact issue stated. When done with the Ability technique you can find the Aspect in play and run the DAC procedure.

We have addressed narrow time periods, like "My rebellious time as a teenager", "my marriage with ex-wife", "my time at the stressful workplace", etc. We find specific situations and then the Aspect that springs from that. Actually, this is exactly where we have used DEEP Viewpoint Clearing. We can in other words replace DVC with DAC if the person so desires and can run it with benefits.

We would probably still run the Ability levels (Grades), each technique to its end point, and take up any Aspects and issues that pop up afterwards. We would actually run an ability level technique and as a result expose Aspects related to the ability we work on. . An Ability Level addresses a specific ability (or disability) and exposes and deals with it in number of ways. We have extensively used Frank A. Gerbode's Ability Enhancement levels. They address in turn Help; Control; Communication; Problems; Misdeeds and Withholding; Upsets; and Fixed Ideas (Rightness level).

We would still run incidents with DEEP Incident Clearing as a separate action. Incident running and regression is a group of techniques that stands the test of time. It is so close to how we think and live. We naturally think back on good and bad times; on happy times and traumatic times. Incident running clears up the stressful and traumatic times.

Any incident that lingers after it has been thoroughly run can however subsequently be addressed with DAC. The lingering material simply indicates that we have to dig deeper into the bosom to find it. Since it can be felt and sensed by the person, it is giving itself away. Address it as a Deep Awareness and you will get to the root of the 'infection'. This 'infection' is the highly personalized reaction that happens in the person's energy body.

The list method (a list of buttons and triggers related to a certain subject, such as intimate relationships, money, being in groups, etc.), could be used. You will find many such lists in the Appendix of first book, 'DEEP Clearing – Releasing the Power of Your Mind'. Using such lists for starters, you will find Aspects related to all kinds of general areas and issues.

Making lists related to Ability levels would be a supplement to those levels and actions.

It would certainly be one technique that should be included. Important general Abilities and subject areas that are covered in Dr. Gerbode's Applied Meta-Psychology are:

Help;
Control;
Communication;
Problems;
Misdeeds: bad conscience, misdeeds (done and received) and holding oneself back;

Upsets: past major upsets;
Fixed ideas and conditions.
Fixed ideas and fixed conditions are general themes all along – even before we get to it as an Ability level or grade.

Addressing, say, Communication with DAC could simply be an additional technique added to the ability level. You would first run all the existing techniques, keeping an eye on Aspects and special issues emerging. You keep a log of all these related special issues. At the appropriate time you would use this list of issues.

So you can use a canned list of key words covering bad communication situations and to that you would add the individual list you have put together during the running of the Ability level on communication.

The Button List System
What would be good key-words on each of the Ability levels?

Here are some suggested lines. It is only meant as inspiration and not as a final version. With most clients there are important sub-areas, as explained, that should be explored in great detail.

We would assess a list and have the person rate each item for charge as we go along. We do recall on charged items found, like: "Recall a situation where you didn't want help." You just run this to find the real charged situation. In this way you pinpoint a key situation, a highly charged incident. Now you can find the Aspect and run DAC on it. Here are the lists:

Help

- "I don't want help"
- "If you want something done, you have to do it yourself."
- "To receive help makes me feel powerless and humiliated."
- "If I receive help I owe the person something."
- "Receiving help makes it too personal."
- "Leave me alone, I am doing fine."
- "They are going to screw it up if I give them the task to do."
- "I think he wants to trick me."
- "If it sounds too good to be true it probably isn't true."
- "It sounds too good to be true."
- "I have lost trust in others."
- "They only want to 'help' to steal my money."
- "They are totally egoistic when it comes to doing work for me."
- "They are only interested in the money."
- "Can I believe what he promises or is it just hot air?"
- "He/she never keeps his promises."
- "I have been let down one time too many."
- "Is he a con man?"
- "If I help they will just take advantage of me."

- "If I help it becomes too personal."
- "I tried to help but got nothing in return."
- "I tried to help but got myself in trouble."

Control

- "I have to control everything."
- "Control is evil."
- "Control means suppression."
- "Controlling people are impossible to be around."
- "Controlling people are ruthless."
- "Controlling people just want to dominate and take over."
- "I will leave the control to the boss."
- "When I try to control something I get scolded."
- "When I try to control a situation I get attacked."
- "I have to stay in control at all times."
- "If I lose control they will get me."

Communication

- Embarrassment
- Afraid of making a fool of yourself
- Afraid of being scolded or punished
- You lack words for what you want to say
- Afraid of what the other person will think or say
- Afraid of being looked down at
- You will attract too much attention
- May cause something that goes out of control
- Afraid the other will discover that you disagree
- You may lose your temper and lose a friend
- If you open up they will see you are vulnerable
- What you want to say is politically incorrect
- What you have to say is in conflict with the other person's beliefs
- What you have to say will make the other person think less of you
- What you have to say will lower your status
- What you have to say will isolate you
- You may say something stupid
- If you speak up you will expose yourself as an outcast
- Fear of losing even the low status you have
- It's better not to rock the boat
- It's better to stay anonymous
- What is on your mind has never been taken up before
- What you have to say will make you look strange and vulnerable
- What you have to say will cause hostilities
- I have no right to speak

- The other is too powerful
- The other controls my food and shelter
- I have a role and status and I won't risk that
- My low status is better than no status
- Etc., etc.

Problems

- You cannot make up your mind
- There are unknowns in the situation
- Things are too complex
- If you make a move it will cause new problems
- It's better to do nothing
- "I will simply wait and see"
- It's too much work and effort
- "I will never succeed"
- If you start on that you will have to realize you have been wrong
- You don't really want to start all over
- It's better to just go with the program
- You are afraid of consequences
- You are afraid of other people's reaction
- You are afraid of that exposing the real problem will get you fired or loss of status
- After all, things are working if you don't change anything
- It's better to let someone else make the decisions
- Etc., etc.

Past misdeeds -- Withholding self. Lying. Shame, blame and regret. Screw ups. Hostilities. Vendetta Sequences

- Withholding self
- Something you are embarrassed about
- Something you regret
- Something you are ashamed of
- Something you couldn't tell others about
- Something that would lower your professional reputation
- Something family members shouldn't know about you
- Something your colleagues or classmates shouldn't know about
- Something that never should come out
- Something your church, the priest or congregation would think was awful
- Something you would never tell
- Something you don't tell the truth about
- Lying about something to family and friends
- Keeping up the façade rather than telling the truth
- A screw-up you were involved in
- Something that went awfully wrong

- Something that shouldn't happen again
- Some situation you were involved in but you regret what you did
- Secret habits or regular activities
- Hostilities towards certain people
- Hate certain people
- Hostilities towards certain groups
- Hate certain groups
- You are at war with certain groups or people
- You want to "pay back" what was done to you
- They deserve the bad luck that they got
- Someone offended you or cheated you and it's payback time
- You cheated someone and it was justified
- You offended someone and it was justified
- You shortchanged someone or gave bad service to them
- Taking advantage of people or situations
- Feeling guilty

Past upsets

- Somebody offended you
- Somebody upset you
- A major negative change happened in your life
- Somebody ridiculed you
- A sweetheart broke off the relationship
- Somebody died
- You got fired
- You flunked a test
- You missed a big opportunity
- You missed an important appointment
- Somebody gossiped about you
- Somebody tried to ruin your reputation
- Somebody attacked you for no or little reason
- Somebody treated you unfairly
- Somebody would never listen to what you had to say
- Somebody would never acknowledge or validate what you had done
- A sweetheart cheated on you
- Somebody cheated you in a deal
- Somebody stole from you
- Somebody robbed you
- Somebody tried to ruin your life or career
- Somebody never did what they promised
- Somebody sabotaged what you were trying to do
- You discovered that all your efforts were of no use
- Someone just wouldn't help you

- Cut off from friends and daily routines (like moving to another city)
- Become sick and have to give up the good life you had
- Having an accident and life as you knew it is not possible

Fixed Ideas

As part of DAC, fixed ideas are covered as we go along. If more work is needed, Fixed Ideas lists can be tailor-made from the knowledge you have of the client. Areas of special interest are repeated bad situations the person finds him- or herself in, over and over, and never seems to learn from. You list out possible and impossible ideas the person may be operating on and assess them for commenting.

When dealing with fixed ideas, one should not forget areas of apparent stupidity, inability or inferiority. Here negative beliefs, or negative Dictates as we call them in DEEP, are in play. The person has accepted negative 'convictions' about own worth or ability. Usually they are generalities, stressful outcries or blunt name-calling. They, most likely, stem from traumatic incidents and overwhelms where the person accepted and adopted these emotional Dictates as 'truths'. It can be denigrating statements from teachers, parents, leaders, seniors, etc. Or it can be short-termed bad solutions to emergencies or traumatic situations. It can even be wrong diagnoses from health-care personnel, including psychologists. You could, of course, ask: "What do you use to make yourself smaller?" or "What has someone else used to make you smaller?" to get the door opened a little bit to this section of the case. But making a list of likely and unlikely statements the person seems to use to beat self over the head is a more thorough method. You assess it in a neutral fashion for comments (slow assessment). By 'neutral' we mean a non-accusative and casual way as it would apply to all humans as possibilities. We bring a Fixed Ideas List related to money to convey the idea; but the clearer will have to make the lists needed for other areas when they are needed.

Fixed Ideas Lists, Money

- I always lose
- Money is made to spend
- Maybe I am lucky today
- I can't have money
- I don't understand finance.
- I will leave dealing with finances to someone else (husband, etc.)
- Money is the root of all evil
- Money is only for the rich
- Expensive things are not for people like us
- You have to sweat to earn money
- I have to spend money to get any status with people
- I have to show them I can afford anything
- I have to buy their affection
- A penny saved is a penny earned
- I won't spend any money
- Money is hard to get by
- The bankers are crooks
- I have to beg to get money

- I will do anything for money
- You don't talk about money
- Money ruins any romance
- Bankers cannot be trusted
- They just want to short change you
- They are trying to cheat you out of your money
- You only get rich by cheating others
- To be rich is to be a profiteer
- Middlemen are parasites
- Money rules the world
- The rich get richer the poor get poorer

In General

We can use Repeated Recall to find charged situations and then take up the charged moments with DAC;

or we can slow assess (using lists from appendix of my first book) and do DEEP Subject Clearing on the relevant and charged lines; then use DAC on key moments that didn't seem to discharge.

We can of course also do assessments and then Recall to find the key incidents and moments to apply DAC to.

Each of the above methods would be valid methods as we see it now.

The standard method we have the most positive experiences with is

1. Do a slow assessment to find a line that is charged and has interest.
2. Do Repeated Recall using the line in some form to find such a highly charged situation.
3. Do DAC on the charged situation.

Chapter 6
Four Stage Releasing

Synopsis – Four Stage Releasing

This new tech is very effective in removing the exact barriers blocking a specific issue. It addresses the exact limiting (reactive) thoughts; the negative emotions and disturbing feelings; unpleasant body-sensations; and various types of impulses and automatic reactions that make the issue reactive, stuck and "unsolvable". All this reactivity, mainly unknown to the person, is located in mind and body and addressed and released in a simple but effective way.

What makes Four Stage Releasing Unique

On top of that the action addresses the spiritual side – what we call the Hidden Data Cloud or Reactive Data Cloud. These are subtle energies that comprise an outdated highly reactive "warning system" stemming from traumas. Some of this energy is of our own making and some of it has attached itself by resonance. Our own side is identical with what we in DEEP call the Repressed Mind (the traumatic content in the subconscious). The attachment part is also known as the entity case. The handling of all this in the new approach is elegant and surprisingly quick. We simply address these energies as a Reactive Data Cloud that is simple to remove by what seems magic. We examine the energies a bit and then simply pull them off in one quick swoop. By this action we have removed the deeper causes of an apparently "handled situation" that mysteriously returned – often again and again.

This spiritual technology is developed by Marc B. Rüedi under the full name of Four Stage Release Rundown. We have been trained directly by Marc.

The Ability One Group has been delivering it as a service. We call it Four Stage Releasing. It aligns very well with the theory of DEEP as laid out in our book "DEEP Clearing – Releasing the Power of Your Mind". Marc's approach is still unique and highly effective. It is especially a breakthrough in handling the hidden reactive thoughts and the Reactive Energy Cloud, including the entity case.

Four Stage Releasing and Life Experience

The following is a write-up based on Marc Rüedi's Four Stage Release Rundown.

We have adjusted the write-up to DEEP Clearing terminology and basics.

We follow the step-by-step protocol developed by Marc Rüedi but use DEEP tools and techniques to release the charged items and issues found. We see it as an action that can take a few sessions for an issue to resolve. We follow the Rules of Clearing closely and this may simply add time. But we also see it as something that adds to the overall benefits. We don't see it as our only goal to simply get rid of the charge of an issue. An equally important goal is to learn from and gain life-experience from what is run. And this is, in our view, best accomplished by giving the client the time he/she needs and give room for him to talk about and compare what comes up to present and past experiences. Repeat and Tell is the workhorse procedure of DEEP and this technique is doing the work. But compared to just bring about a discharge without emphasizing new insights does add time compared to Marc's original approach. Past and more recent situations tend to pop up and the person is given the opportunity to talk it out and see patterns in his or her life and really understand what has been going on and then let go. Each time the person has compared it to life-experiences we do return the person to the original task of perceiving the DEEP element as an energy that is present here and now. Thus we do make sure the live energy is fully released as well.

The Original Technique has Unique Features

The general theory and approach of Four Stage Releasing is the same as in Deep Awareness and Aspect Clearing (DAC). But there are some important differences that make Marc Rüedi's method unique and also very effective – especially the method of removing any remaining reactive energies (The Reactive Data Cloud) as explained later. We have used both methods (DAC and 4-Stage) extensively – but not with enough different clients to say that the one method replaces the other – or if one method is suited for certain issues and clients and the other method is suited for other issues and clients. So we bring both methods here in the same publication and hopefully await feedback from clearers and their experiences with the two methods.

About Four Stage Releasing in General

In this action we do not use detailed lists of questions but are more interested in the energies lodged in the body tissues and the actual local experience of an issue. By 'local' we mean that each body section, such as the Throat, the Heart, the Solar Plexus, the Stomach and the Abdomen has a local experience and certain reactions to an issue. This may be familiar to body workers.

We have earlier encountered and described such phenomena under the heading of DEEP Body Clearing in our basic book. That body parts 'talk' may of course appear strange to some, especially persons who see the intellect as the real person and tend to disregard emotions and feelings as no more than annoyances.

In our experience Four Stage Releasing therefore works best with persons who have a good awareness of what goes on in the body and on the emotional plane in regard to an issue. Still, all these subtle reactions are what comprise Charge – Charge being energies, emotions, sensations and thoughts that are disturbing and react automatically. If they were originally opposed or stopped, these energies get stored in the subconscious energy systems of a human being and can be triggered out of control when we unknowingly are reminded of something from our past experience that was stressful, traumatic or dangerous.

All these reactions, it could be said, make up a sophisticated warning system; a system that sounds the alarm when it perceives that the circumstances of a past threat to survival and well-being is present. Unfortunately, this subconscious warning system works on an extreme 'Better safe than sorry' mode. By this we mean the slightest danger or reminder tends to trigger the alarm even when a rational look at the situation shows that no real danger is present. The system therefore often causes very irrational behaviors and feelings and causes unnecessary mental distress and pain. These mechanisms are fully explained in our first book (and elsewhere) and we can refer students to Chapter 8: Spirit – Mind – Body.

The premise in Four Stage is that all the subtle energies comprising an irrational warning can be contacted one by one and discharged. When that is done successfully phenomena will no longer be triggered automatically. The person will regain the ability to observe and evaluate any situation in a fresh and direct way. Rationality has returned – no reason to simply react; no reason to lose presence of mind and become the victim of or give in to reactivity.

The Thought Level

We hold on to old issues for a reason – usually an unknown and irrational reason buried down deep. These reasons are ways we explain or hold on to our shortcomings and faults. Many of them are justifications; some of them are fixed ideas stemming from traumatic experiences. Finding the limiting thoughts that hold an undesired condition in place is a golden shortcut to lighten the situation considerably when it is possible.

If we are talking about a recent loss or other emotional situation we address the emotional distress first. But if we are talking about issues that have followed and been with the person for a long time it is crucial to find the reactive rationale that makes the person hold on to that.

Issues that can be Taken Up

Practically any issue can be taken up – just like we can with DAC. We need however an issue that has charge and importance for the person for it to run well. If we are talking about recent and ongoing problems, upsets and losses we address the emotional side directly and don't go into the Thought level unless it offers itself to be run. Obviously, the person is not holding on to the issue per se, but is simply working on getting through it. Major losses and upsets in general are more suited for being run as incidents. Issues that are best suited for Four Stage Releasing are personal shortcomings, situations that seem to repeat themselves in a person's life and enduring emotional problems and issues. Body problems can be addressed with the caveat that we do not promise to cure illness but we can alleviate discomforts and sources of stress. We alleviate any bottled up charge that surrounds the issue. A body problem, such as stomach problems, catching colds easily, etc. etc., can simply be taken up as the main issue.

Four Stage Releasing by Steps

We assume the person comes to us to address and handle a specific issue, a shortcoming, a relationship problem or condition in his or her life.

The first step is to get it formulated in a way so it indicates to the person. Also, we have to formulate it in a way so it is something we can actually address. 'No money' is not an issue we can address. But an underlying condition that leads to no money can usually be found and addressed successfully. It could be lack of concentration and motivation, being a shopaholic, being the big spender, hating to make plans, or the like. Here we have formulated the complaint in a way so the person can do something about it – start to take responsibility for it – and we are in business. So step one is:

1. Sort out what issue the person wants to address. As explained above, if it is a recent loss or upset – in other words an emotional issue primarily, address it as such. That is Level 2 of the write-up. If it is a more permanent issue, sort out a formulation that is very real to the person. Find a formulation that indicates. We use the system of a scale from 0-10 (the SUD scale: Subjective Units of Distress), 10 being the most distressful and charged value. Once you have the right issue, it should also be at least 7 on this scale. In Four Stage Releasing we don't find the Aspect. The formulation we find is the issue. It is the issue itself formulated in a subjective way; we are looking for the personal or beingness angle. That is the problem we isolate on this step.

If the person cannot clearly formulate the problem but still is in distress, start with level 2 as well. If the person has difficulties accessing his/her emotions he can usually at least access the body-sensations in the stomach; so simply start there. Once some of the emotions and sensations are released, the person will usually see the situation more clearly and can come up with a usable formulation. Once you have a formulation that indicates and has charge, go back to Level 1 (the thought level) and go through the whole procedure from there, including a fresh look at level 2.

Level 1 – the Thought Level

What we are interested in are the hidden subconscious thoughts. We usually find self-limiting thoughts, generalities etc. that confuses or disables the person's ability to think straight. When such thoughts pop up from the repressed mind we have our material. We ask and instruct the person to report what pops up and are less interested in rational explanations. If the person gives very analytical answers we hear them out but instruct the person to look into the subconscious mind. "Is there anything that just pops up when I ask the question?" is one way to get around the long explanations. Here are the questions we use. We may not need them all but once we have gotten a pop up answer we work it over and release the charge and automaticity of the answer. When we are about done we can however choose to go through all the questions as a final check.

Q1: is there a good reason why you have (that item/issue)?
Q2: is there s/t in yourself that makes it an issue?
Q3: is there a reactive thought that is part of (that issue)?
Q4: is there some way it is good for you to have (the issue)?,
Q5: do you somehow gain from having (the issue)?
Q6: is there somehow a way (the issue) serves you?
Q7: does the (issue) in some way help you?
Q8: is there s/t you would you lose, if you didn't have (that issue) ?
Q9: if the mind would find a reason why it is good for you to have...
(issue) – what would it be?
Q10: is there a decision about "it must not happen again" built into this issue?
Q11: is there a warning signal built into this issue?
Q12: is (issue) a solution that appears as a solution or way out from s/t else?

Pop up answers are handled in the same way as in DAC. You have the person repeat the statement once as he really means it and acknowledge that. This is done a few times. Then you can have the person repeat the answer in different moods – on different tone levels. If the statement sounds like a dictate or command phrase the person may have adopted from an authority figure, have him find the character saying it; have the person then say it from that viewpoint. You can also ask into if he really means it or it makes sense to him. At some point the person may just laugh off the statement as nonsense or non-applicable and that means you are done.

Note: there are other tools in DEEP tool box, such as running opposites 'Get the idea of (statement A)'. 'Get the idea of (statement minus A)'; or running 'How has it helped you?' 'How has it harmed you?'

Sometimes the person cannot let go of the validity of a thought. This is an indicator of a deeper issue. We should look for a deeper and more existential problem, a problem that is closer to the person's timeless beingness, so to speak. A 'problem dealing with the opposite sex' can reveal 'shyness' as the underlying issue. Shyness is a beingness or character problem and not a situation problem and therefore a more pervasive aberration. If you encounter that, you should restate the issue as soon as there is an opportunity after completing whatever action you are working on. You can simply ask, "Is Shyness the underlying issue?" and if Yes. Ask, "Is it ok if we restate the issue as Shyness?" and if accepted you use the new formulation going forward.

Level 2 - Feelings

Level 2 is about finding emotions, feelings, sensations, etc. – all the DEEP items that are lodged in the body in relation to the issue. This sometimes includes thoughts, impulses and efforts. We go through the body in a systematic way, starting with the Heart. You ask the person to be in the Heart when doing this step. Sample question:

"How does your Heart feel about (issue)?"

You get emotions, feelings, sensations mainly; occasionally also thoughts and impulses. If something pops up in a different part of the body, e.g. the abdomen, you take it up right away and release the charge; then you return to the Heart-question. You work over the Heart area until no more answers come up. In this way you work your way through Heart (as explained); then Abdomen; Stomach; Solar-plexus; Chest; Throat/Jaws. Each time something pops up you flatten it with Repeat and Tell and other DEEP tools. Then you scan the areas, just to make sure to catch new DEEP elements that possibly were triggered during the process: Abdomen; Stomach; Solar-plexus; Chest and Heart; Throat/Jaws.

Now we do a full body scanning. We start at the toes and go step by step to top of head. Take it section by section: right foot, right lower leg, right knee, right thigh etc. Both right and left side this way and all the way up to the top of the head. Anything that pops up is released with DEEP tools right away.

If you encounter resistive feelings, etc. we can use the tool of shining a light into the area and/or expand the area and thus making the energy less dense. "Shine a yellow or white light into the area where that feeling is sitting." "Take that area and make it larger and less dense. Simply make it bigger and bigger so the energy is being diluted", are sample instructions. You can also ask the person to ground the feeling. "From where the feeling is sitting in your body, make a connection to the earth; likewise, make a connection to your higher self or to a higher power." This simply grounds and connects the area and can be helpful in discharging an area.

Level 3 – Survival Instincts

Here we are dealing with the Fight – Flee – Freeze reactions that are well-known from biology and psychology. Facing danger we can react by fighting the danger; we can react by running away from the danger; or we can 'play dead' – freeze – and hope not to be noticed or seen as dead by the aggressor or predator. These automatic reactions can be lodged deeply in the body and brainstem (the survival brain) in relation to a certain issue. And even if we could also describe them as feelings, addressing them directly and by name has time and again proven to be very valuable. Such reactions can be so engrained in our behavior so we have stopped noticing them as a special condition. Yet, when addressed and released it can be a life-changing moment.

In FOUR STAGE RELEASING, we first discuss if any Fight – Flee – Freeze reactions were connected to the issue at hand. Usually you will find all three at one point or another of any issue. We discuss fight, flee, freeze situations loosely. When we take them up for real we start with the Freeze reaction however. We run it as an imaginary thing. Can you imagine yourself freezing in the situation; playing dead; becoming invisible. Then you do a similar action with Flee and Fight. You have the person imagining such a situation. Besides Fight – Flee – Freeze we have experimented with adding Hide (as a form of freeze) and Pray (asking for mercy) that could be seen as a reaction if the freeze didn't work. Despite your best efforts you have been discovered and the predator is ready to attack you. You ask for mercy as a last ditch effort to save your skin.

Oftentimes running Survival Instincts has resulted in that for instance a permanent freeze or flee reaction has been spotted and released. This is often encountered in people suffering from chronic fear.

Attachment by Resonance

One thing that makes FOUR STAGE RELEASING unique is the addressing of the attachment case. What exactly do we mean by that?

The basis of a person's case is the traumatic experiences a person has undergone – not only this life-time but also in countless existences prior to the present life. It is, as we have pointed out repeatedly, especially the subjective reactions in these traumatic experiences that make a permanent imprint on the person. All these experiences and all our subjective reactions to them have roughened up our energy field. And we are holding on to these disturbances, it seems, in order to use them as part of a warning system. Should anything similar happen again our subconscious 'radar' will detect them in time and we can avoid a repeat of the situation.

But the bottom line is that we now have an energy-field with many odd characteristics in terms of disturbances, content and the wave-patterns of all of this. These very complex content patterns of waves, frequencies, experiences and memories have the characteristics of an electromagnetic field: It will, piece by piece, attract alike energies. We have the Law of Attraction: Like will attract like. This is true on a macro-level, in our daily lives and what people, situations, fortunes and misfortunes we run into. It is however also true on an energetic level. The universe is full of free floating energies that were created in the past sometime and now are floating around – apparently without a home, without clear ownership and without a clear source. These energies will attach to like frequencies and their content. So when we deal with the Resonance- or Attachment-case we are dealing with this 'Cloud' that our own case has attracted and we now can find attached to it.

So the Resonance-case has two ingredients. There is our own side and there is the foreign side. Our own side is our own warning system with all the traumatic content in a light form. It doesn't necessarily bother us because it is so light; it is mainly data that are not energized. It is like a blueprint, an empty radar screen that reflects the environment. Marc compares it with an antivirus program on a computer. It runs all the time but only goes into action if a computer virus is encountered.

If this mechanism gets triggered it becomes energized and that is how we get all these odd reactions in our field. That is all the emotions, feelings, thoughts, body-sensations etc. that we have dealt with so far in FOUR STAGE RELEASING. What we need to do now is to identify these blueprints, the radar mechanism itself. We locate the relevant blueprint and all the attached energies. Once located we can now deal with both sides: Our own side – the blueprint – and all the energies that have been attached to it by resonance. The collective energy-phenomenon is what we call the Reactive Data Cloud – and that is what we deal with in Step 4.

Level 4 – The Reactive Data Cloud

Let us summarize. The Reactive Data Cloud consists of our own subconsciously recorded information, the blueprints. Add to that the attached energies and masses coming from the outside – the attachment case. The two sides tend to deadlock against each other and thus stay in place. When we work with it, it can be hard to tell the two sides apart. "What is my own stuff and what has come from the outside?" It has usually been around for so long and thus just seems to be 'how it is to be me.' But we have now already released most of our own charge on the prior steps; we have carefully worked our way backwards and released most of the active energies of the issue.

But now we have finally come to a data or information level that precedes the charge we have handled so far. It is perceivable as a fine energy in or around the body. It usually attaches itself to a body part and this can be perceived as a light pressure. The Cloud can be located above or around the body; but sometimes it is inside and attaching itself to the heart, solar-plexus or another organ.

Our task at hand is to locate this Reactive Data Cloud and have it released from the person. Since we have handled most of the charge by doing levels 1-3 it usually goes quite easily. We are only dealing with remnants of the original charge. At this stage we can characterize it and deal with it as light energy-phenomena. We mainly pay attention to the attachment case but by doing this, we unsettle the equilibrium between the two sides; and by this action we handle our own 'blueprint' reactivity as well.

Level 4 by Steps

1. Have the person locate the Reactive Data Cloud. It can be outside, around or in the body. If outside, ask **"where is the Cloud attached?"** Direct the person to find a light pressure.

2. Ask **"where does the Cloud come from – when did it attach to you?"**
Work with this step. It could have attached in early childhood or several or many lifetimes ago. It could even be 'before time'. Work it back and forth until the person seems certain. Have him identify loosely what happened at that time.

3. Then: **"Go back to a time before that Cloud existed."** You have him find a neutral position on the timeline in the past. It could be a historic event or just any time prior where this energy wasn't present and not bothering him.

4. Now you use below questions to get the person to contemplate the influence this Cloud has had on his life and existence. What the person answers is of less importance. The main idea is to have the person contemplate the Cloud and realize how it has affected him.

"Go into your Heart and get what you need to learn from this
- what does my Heart want to teach me?"
"What am I NOW DOING that once I let this energy go I will stop doing?"
"What am I now NOT DOING that once I let this energy go I will start doing?"

5. Removing the Reactive Data Cloud
"Are you 100% willing to let go of this energy – are you willing to do it now?"
If yes: **Intend a Higher Self to help and say aloud.**
"I ask for this energy to be removed" and let it discharge fully.

Give it some time. It normally discharges slower for the person than it seems to the clearer. Then ask:

"What happened – did the energy leave?"

Here it is important to HAVE the Cloud removed rather than asking the person to remove it or try to remove it as a clearer. We are asking for assistance from a higher power so no egos gets involved.

6. There are several scenarios in case the Cloud didn't leave.

There can be several strands (parts) of the Cloud and we have only gotten part of it. Or we can have gotten a wrong date for what we took up. Those are the most common problems.

You can ask: **"Is there an additional strand (part) to that Reactive Data Cloud?"**

If so, you deal with it by dating and removing.

If you suspect a wrong date for the Cloud taken up, you can simply check, **"Is there a wrong date for the Cloud?"** and if so, redo the dating and the removal.

If the person absolutely won't let go of the Cloud it can simply be because it is of his own making, his own energy and part of his case. In that case, you discuss it as an issue and then take it up, starting with Stage 1, the thought level. You have to find the justifications for holding on to it. Sample question: "Why is it good for you to have (that Cloud)?" (See also note 2)

You also check (as a final test) if the person feels the Cloud is fully gone. If not, it usually means one of the above problems is still unhandled, such as an additional strand. You keep handling the Cloud till the person is happy and satisfied that it has been removed completely.

Note 1: there could be parallel strands that turn up in a day – or later. It will however be a different energy although similar. Should it happen the charge is simply handled in session as additional strands.

Note 2: the person may insist that the Cloud is all his own energy. In such a case it is usually a mixture of own and foreign energies. Explain to the person that the Cloud can be a sandwich between the two and it can be triggered by the person pushing against the foreign energy. Ask the person if that is the case. If yes, tell him that you will first deal with the foreign energy. As this removes the energy the person is holding off by pushing, the whole phenomenon may resolve once there is nothing to push against. If there is still remnants of own side, run level 1 on the energy(Q1: Is there a good reason why you have that energy etc.)

Final Step

There is a final step to FOUR STAGE RELEASING that you may use. It is about creating a new beingness once you have gotten rid of the reactive charge.

1. **"Create a new energy/image/feeling that is who you really are".**

Find out if he likes it.

2. "Look if your heart and see if it accepts it easily and fully."

(If your Heart does not accept it easily you didn't get all the parts of the Reactive Data Cloud yet. Go back and check for another strand of this Cloud) or use the following:

3. (If yes): "Create a ball of this your own energy, big enough for you to sit inside.

Saturate your body with this energy. Ok, now make the ball bigger and bigger.

- And as it becomes bigger it loses its density and becomes thinner and thinner until it vanishes.

Make it as big as your house; your city; country; continent; planet; solar system; universe.

Is the ball gone?"

Once the person can answer in the affirmative that he/she has saturated the space with this new energy we are done with that issue. In the next session another issue can be taken up.

Remember: If the heart does not accept it easily we didn't get all parts of the Cloud yet.

Go back and check for another strand of this Cloud).

Prompt Sheet – Four Stage Releasing

1. Let the person word his problem so it indicates! If he cannot find the problem or has too many, start with the Belly. If he is in an emotional stress situation (like death of a loved one etc.) do an assist – Level 2 Light (just asking for emotions, feelings, sensations). If you are in a session setting, and your communication with the client is good and it is real to the client, you can do full level 2 as an assist (including body).

2 Decide where you want to start - If he has a problem that indicates – check strength 0-10. If 7+ go ahead. - If the person is emotionally charged, start with the emotions.

- If he has no emotions and no thoughts – start with the body-sensations.

<u>3. Level 1 – Hidden Thoughts</u>
Get all the hidden pop-up thoughts, using (as appropriate) one or more of these:

Q1: is there a good reason why you have (that item/issue)?

Q2: is there s/t in yourself that makes it an issue?

Q3: is there a reactive thought that is part of (that issue)?

Q4: is there some way it is good for you to have (the issue)?,

Q5: do you somehow gain from having (the issue)?

Q6: is there somehow a way (the issue) serves you?

Q7: does the (issue) in some way help you?

Q8: is there s/t you would you lose, if you didn't have (that issue) ?

Q9: if the mind would find a reason why it is good for you to have... (issue) – what would it be?

Q10: is there a decision about "it must not happen again" built into this issue?

Q11: is there a warning signal built into this issue?

Q12: is (issue) a solution that appears as a solution or way out from s/t else?

"Ok, repeat this thought aloud, feel its energy and accept it. Listen to yourself saying it". "Say it in a different mood/tone of voice."

Also: Find the Viewpoint/role that would say it and have client say it from that role. Use: "Is it true for you?" "Is it still valid?" Discharge each fully and make sure, the person no longer sees it as valid.

Note: there are other tools in DEEP tool box, such as running opposites 'Get the idea of (statement A)'. 'Get the idea of (statement 'minus A)'; or running 'How has it helped you?' 'How has it harmed you?'

If there is a fixation – if he cannot let go of the validity of the thought – you need to find the underlying, deeper problem – related to his core beingness rather than a situation.

<u>4. Level 2 – Feelings in Heart and Body</u>
Discharge one by one by fully accepting what is there.
'How does your Heart feel about (problem)?
Heart; Belly; Stomach, Solar-plexus/chest; Throat/jaw
Then: Scan those areas: belly, stomach, solar plexus/chest, throat/jaw.
If these are all clean, scan the whole body from toe to top of head.
Tools: Use golden light (lower body and heart) / white light (upper body) if necessary. Make the area bigger and less dense, etc.
Connect the DEEP-energy to earth and to the higher self and let it discharge this way.

5. Level 3 – Survival-Instincts: Fight –Flee–Freeze

Discuss fight-flee-freeze situations and scenarios related to issue.

Discharge by starting with 'Freeze' (if applicable); then 'Flight'; then Fight. Have him play Freeze, 'playing dead, still, not move'; (check 'Hide' if suspected (you would do HIDE before the Freeze); Flee – running far away until you are safe; Fight – big, courageous beingness; lion, fighter or similar being disturbed.

6. Level 4 – Clean out the Reactive Data Cloud.

The reactive data cloud is the reactive blueprint and the hidden energy behind the issue. It is a 'radar mechanism' or 'antivirus program' that can be triggered and energized by the environment at a later date. It consists of one's own reactive side (the blueprint) and the attachment side (energies held by resonance). We mainly address the attachment side on this step as that usually resolves the situation. Own side triggered energies were addressed in detail on steps 1-3.

Let the person find the Reactive Data Cloud where it is, outside, around or in the body. If outside, where could it be attached? (Spot light pressure)

Ask: **"Where does it come from, when did it attach to you?"** (Get date and outline of situation).

(Note: it is often longer ago than he sees at first). Check for 'is it older?':

"Did you have it at birth? – Did you have it in earlier life-times – how many?"

Then: **"Go back before this energy was ever created"** (are you there?)

Note: Many of these energies are very, very old). You go before that (or to a place where this energy did not yet exist) – might be 'before time'.

Then ask the below questions (need not answer – just contemplate):

"Go into your heart and get what you need to learn from this.
- What does my heart want to teach me?"

"What am I NOW DOING, that once I let this energy go I will stop doing?"
"What am I now NOT DOING that once I let this energy go I will start doing?"

7 Remove the Cloud:

"Are you 100% willing to let go of this energy – are you willing to do this now?"

If yes: intend Higher Self to help and say out loud:

"I ask for this energy to be removed" and let it discharge fully.

Give it some time – it normally discharges slower for the person than it seems to the clearer. Then ask **"What happened – did the energy leave?"**

If not all gone

Re-date the time when it attached and re-date its age and let the person go before this energy had ever been created.

Go from there. (Often it then dissolves quickly.)

Check if the problem you started with is now fully cleaned out. (Strength should be ZERO). Check it by feeling into an old, formerly very charged incident where he had this problem. Check it also in the future: "Do you think it could come back?" If so – there is more to be cleaned out: check for remaining Reactive Data Clouds' and clean them out.

Note 1: there could be parallel strands that turn up in a day – or later. It will however be a different energy although similar. Should it happen the charge is simply handled in session as additional strands.

Note 2: the person may insist that the Cloud is all his own energy. In such a case it is usually a mixture of own and foreign energies. Explain to the person that the energy most likely is a sandwich between the two and it is triggered by the person pushing against the foreign energy. Tell him that you will first deal with the foreign energy. As this removes the energy the person is holding off by pushing, the whole phenomenon may resolve once there is nothing to push against. If there is still remnants of own side, run level 1 on the energy (Q1: Is there a good reason why you have that energy? etc.)

Final Step – "Create a new energy/image/feeling that is who you really are".

Find out if he likes it**. "Look if your heart accepts it easily."**

Note: If the heart does not accept it easily we didn't get all parts of the Cloud yet.

Go back and check for another strand of this Cloud)'.

If all OK: **"create a ball with this your own energy, big enough to sit inside the ball, saturate your body with this energy. Ok, now make this ball bigger and bigger – and as it becomes bigger it loses its density and becomes thinner and thinner until it vanishes. Make it as big as the house, your city, your country, your continent, planet earth, the universe.... Is the ball gone?"**

Four Stage Releasing:

Using the Chakras as Reference Points

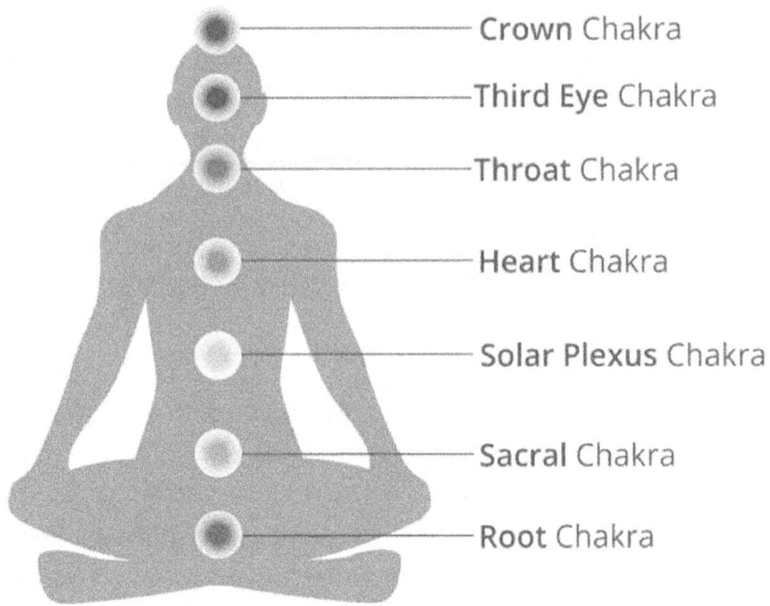

It has been suggested to use the chakras as reference points when checking for DEEP elements in the body. This seems to work very well with people that are familiar the chakra system. This is not part of the original FOUR STAGE RELEASING or the way it is taught by Marc Rüedi. But with people who think in these terms and have used chakras in other contexts we would think it is productive.

In the original version we check Heart; Stomach; Abdomen; Solar Plexus; Chest; Throat/Jaws for emotions, feelings and body-sensations. This has usually triggered reactions in all the chakra areas. And as stated in the materials, we take up anything that is triggered. With most, that covers all the chakras in torso and throat.

Using the chakras we would check the Heart chakra; Solar Plexus chakra; Sacral Chakra; Root chakra; Throat chakra; and in addition Third Eye chakra and Crown chakra. For most people, as said, it would produce the same material. But Root chakra, Third Eye chakra and Crown chakra are not specifically covered in the original list of reference points. For some the Root chakra will produce new material. The Third Eye and Crown chakra may or may not produce feelings, emotions or body-sensations. But it is suggested that they may produce intangible feelings, thoughts and ideas related to the issue. When that is the case they are simply released with the techniques described for releasing thoughts and feelings – mainly by Repeat and Tell. We don't go into a detailed description of what the different chakras are supposed to contain or stand for. The general principle of DEEP has been that we ask the person to LOOK without any preconceived ideas. Therefore we leave it at that but leave the door open to experiment with it.

Chapter 7: GPM Series 1

GPM Series 1: DEEP Character Clearing – Basic Concepts

Note: For special terms in the GPM Series, see special glossary in the appendices. The GPM series was done based on some inspirational but incomplete research done by Ron Hubbard. DEEP Character Clearing is our attempt to complete this research of an important part of the case. We have used much of Hubbard's terminology which in general lies outside DEEP Clearing. Thus there is a need for that special glossary.

In a troubled relationship there are some hidden factors that make the situation worse. We tend to slip into roles and respond irrationally. One could of course look at each upset or conflict to sort it out. In ***DEEP Character Clearing*** we are, however, looking for one of the root causes. In the illustration we see what happens in the woman's mind. She has a package of images, energy-masses and ideas about angry men and one of herself responding. Each package is called an *Identity (ID)*. In certain types of conflicts, these two reactive identities are at work. The woman will project her negative 'blue angry man identity' onto the person in front of her. He appears 'all blue'. She will react to this 'blue man' according to her own 'red angry woman identity'.

Using *DEEP Character Clearing* the woman can have her own mind cleared of the two irrational and clashing identities. Once that is done, the actual relationship will change dramatically as well.

In *DEEP Character Clearing* we find these identities as energy-masses (mental ridges) in the mind. We process each of them separately. The first step is to find the troublesome Identity in opposition (the counter-pole or ID2). The woman can be asked to think of a specific conflict with the man. She is asked questions in order to locate the apparent energy-mass that represents the man in the conflict. She is asked to describe or draw its shape and impact on the body as it appears to her. She finds a few characteristics to describe how that role feels. The energy-mass can be perceived to be anywhere; inside or outside the body; near or far away; around the head or elsewhere. Once the basic characteristics of this mental energy-mass are established, one can find the decisions, emotions, energies and polarities that role operates on.

The name DEEP derives from that as it stands for: Decisions, Emotions, Energies and Polarities, and these are the elements the practitioner can isolate and discharge in these identities, resulting in the IDs losing their power to irrationally control the client or to interfere in the relationship.

Finding and discharging the "blue man" counter-pole is thus the first step. Once that is done, the woman can be that role without losing her temper — or leave it alone at will.

Next, we find the energy-mass that represents herself in the conflict (Own ID, ID1). An *Identity* contains a whole package of experiences and incidents going way back in time. All this has been organized into an Identity to make it quickly and easily available. It became an identity, as the woman adopted a whole set of emotions, responses and fixed ideas to use in similar situations. It has to some degree taken on a life of its own. This can be very subtle — yet it can be found in the best of us without fail. One reason the two identities persist, is that they hang up against each other in an unresolved conflict or games-condition. They are both "right" and are blind when it comes to seeing the situation from the other point of view.

There is a series of steps in *DEEP Character Clearing,* all designed to dissolve the two identities as energy-masses. Once the steps are successfully done, the woman can suddenly see her counter-pole for what he really is. She can now communicate directly with the person. She has no need to use or project the blue energy-mass onto the man. It acted as prejudice and mental name calling. As a rule the counter-pole is a dehumanized, demonized or grossly distorted version of the actual person.

Likewise, she can be herself without slipping into the red side of the problem. She can therefore *take the lead in resolving problems* between them in a rational manner.

By using the various *DEEP Character Clearing techniques*, all kinds of new and old conflicts are being addressed. Also turbulent periods of a person's life can be addressed as the confusion contained therein consisted of viewpoints in conflict.

The Super Problems Process

One technique within DEEP Character Clearing is called *the Super Problems Process.* Here we take up a subject the client is passionate about. We find all the goals and identities in conflict or opposition to each other within that certain area, be it "marriage", "study", "religion", "collecting stamps", "football", "health", "enforcing the law", etc. We can address any subject the client is passionate about, one after the other. Processing the area has a powerful outcome — just like it happens in an Italian opera if the plot comes to a happy ending: All the efforts and characters come together in the grand finale having learned to live and work together. They can sing the same tune with one powerful voice!

As a result of the various DEEP Character Clearing techniques, unwanted conditions, physical and emotional, are routinely alleviated. Often forgotten or innocent looking conflicts from childhood are found and reveal heavy disturbances in the energy field. Processing them, using *DEEP Character Clearing*, can turn the key and unlock troubled relationships and unwanted conditions. New circumstances in life may reveal dormant energy-masses that can be addressed right away. At some point, all available energy-masses have been resolved *using a number of DEEP techniques*. The woman will have reached a state of clarity of mind, of having thoroughly cleansed her energy field. She will have grown as a spiritual Being as a result. She will be much more able to enjoy life. She can meet any adversity with an open mind and a resolve that makes it seem like a game she is willing to play.***Note:*** *in this day and age of equal opportunity and equality among the sexes, the above example may seem inappropriate to some. We assure you, we are not taking a stand for inequality. We have used the example because it seems effective in getting the basic concept across. This is because we all have known men and women who are operating in these traditional roles of the sexes. Please note: this type of processing is actually intended as an effective way to overcome any type of "traditional roles."*

Chapter 8: GPM Series 2

The "Lost" Tech of Actual GPMs

Early on there is plenty to take up on a case. The person has all kinds of stressful and traumatic situations to work through. This is what we address in 'Life-Repair' and the so-called Grades. Following the line-up of the Grade Chart, the goal for the case is to go clear. Again, following the Grade Chart we get to the more advanced levels after clear, called the OT levels. If we follow Ron Hubbard's research line, however, there is an important part of the case that now is being completely overlooked. The Actual GPMs, the archetypical conflicts and games that have formed our destiny and character throughout time. GPM stands for Goals-Problems-Mass. These case phenomena were in the 1960s described as being at the core of the case. Maybe they still are?

If you look closely at this core, you find a series of goals and identities or sub-personalities the person is currently operating on. In addition, there is a supply of past goals and identities. Among them are very basic goals as well as more practical and contemporary ones. Each goal you find is running on a cycle of action, it has its own unique Be-Do-Have. The Be was the identity, role or "hat" assumed in order to operate. The Do is the execution of the goal. The Have is the desired end result. For example, the identity could be 'police man' (be). The goal could be 'to enforce the law' (do). The desired end result would be 'lawful-ness' (have). Goals that are fulfilled successfully cease to exert any influence as they are completed cycles. However, goals that are incomplete, due to their basic nature or their vastness -- or abandoned due to the opposition they met, tend to remain with the individual at some level. Over time, these incomplete or abandoned goals group in a certain way. They become part of what is called a Goals-Problems-Mass (GPM, see below). Since these goals and identities, at some point, were chosen consciously by the person and happily pursued for a long, long time as "my life" they have a great capability to influence and aberrate the person and go into action, even after they are long "forgotten" on a conscious level.

Anatomy of a GPM

An Actual GPM consists of such own goals and goals that opposes them. We have and postulate goals to have a game. Once postulated they may attract opponents. This brings about a pair of goals, also called a dichotomy. You could say a dichotomy is an old or current unresolved conflict or games-condition that produces charge between the two sides. One identity with its goal acts like a pole in a battery. The one side of the dichotomy is the person's own goal. The other side is the opposition that eventually frustrated the person to a degree so he/she abandoned pursuing the goal. One such abandoned conflict is being layered on top of the next as time goes on. The goals in the dichotomy clash so they form problems and masses in the person's mind. These masses can remain with the individual for millennia. The basic anatomy of a problem is goal-counter goal; intention-counter intention; or one confusion that is hung up against another comparable but opposing confusion. The basic goals the person pursued are typically very broad and general as remote guiding stars that lead a person in a certain general direction. These goals align themselves along our basic spheres and ways of existence (the dynamics) such as our personal life, our family life, our group life etc. These dynamics are by themselves very basic goals in this universe. An example of a goal would be "to obtain wealth". To succeed, all the opportunities and strategies of life may come into play and countless related incidents happen and accumulate. Sub-goals and corresponding "hats" or identities are taken on in order to succeed. You can probably imagine the opposition and counter-goals the person runs into during this general pursuit and all the "hats" he/she needs to wear in order to succeed.

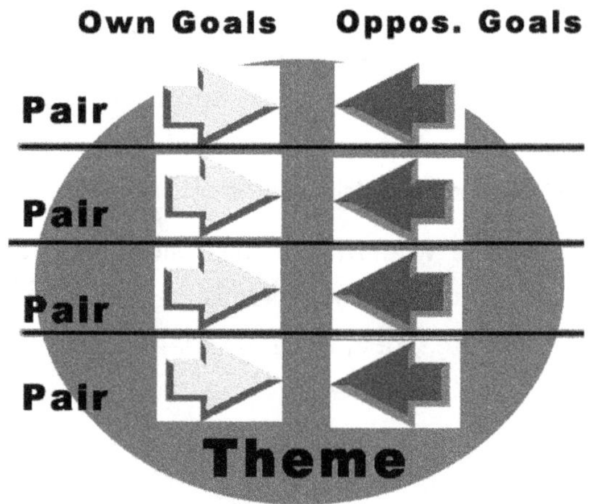

A GPM consists of pairs of opposing goals, one pair is layered on top of the next over time. All goals have one theme in common. That's the playing field or what the two sides fight over. One can start by finding such a theme that is in play in one's life, then one goal related to that theme and what opposes it. One would then find another goal and its opposition, repeatedly until all available polarities are discharged. Both the goals and the IDs behind them have to be skillfully discharged as one goes along.

Early Research

The subject of Goals-Problems-Mass was first researched by Ron Hubbard between 1961-65. The processes developed during that period were, however, highly experimental. Although much data was accumulated during the original research, no safe technique emerged that could be put in general use. There is one exception to this. The 1965 process known as "Routine 6 End-words" looks at light reminders on the Actual GPMs and can lead to some relief. It is safe (but not that effective) and is used as Grade 6 (before the Clearing Course) in the grade chart of 1965-1978.

Actual GPMs are different from Implant GPMs. Implant GPMs are short (traumatic (engramic) incidents where the person was subjected to overwhelm (usually by electronic means) while being loaded with a long series of conflicting goals. This was a mind control operation (intense "brain washing") performed to confuse an individual and reduce his power and clarity of mind into that of a more subdued, controllable and dumb individual.

Implant GPMs can also be run out and examples of that would be advanced level OT-2, the original Clearing Course materials, Helatrobus Implants and others.

An Actual GPM is sometimes described as a perceivable black mass or mist that is located in the vicinity of the person. There are numerous GPMs on a person's case. Each GPM is held together by a subject matter (theme). All goals and identities in the GPM are closely related to this theme. The pairs of opposing goals also relate to each other in a pattern known as the Line Plot. Since the Line Plot is not used in the procedure we will not describe it in great detail here. We will just say that once a goal has been pursued for a long time in life the person hits a dead end. He is burned out due to the opposition. He therefore reinvents his pursuit but on a slightly less ambitions level. He uses this "tactic" to try to overcome the opposition first met. In this way, he will in turn pursue a series of goals related to the same subject matter, each in turn opposed by the environment (usually other beings) and each eventually coming to a halt when the person gets stuck doing it, prompting a new lower scaled goal. You can plot the deterioration of ambition on various scales. Eventually he will abandon the subject matter entirely, once he has reached bottom, and start a new series of goals related to a new theme. Although the Line Plot isn't part of the procedure, it is worth noticing that once a GPM is formed it sets out a pattern that later can be dramatized. The person may click into the succession of goals and contra goals, as if it were a play or set of rails to follow, and go through the whole gamut within a short or long period of time.

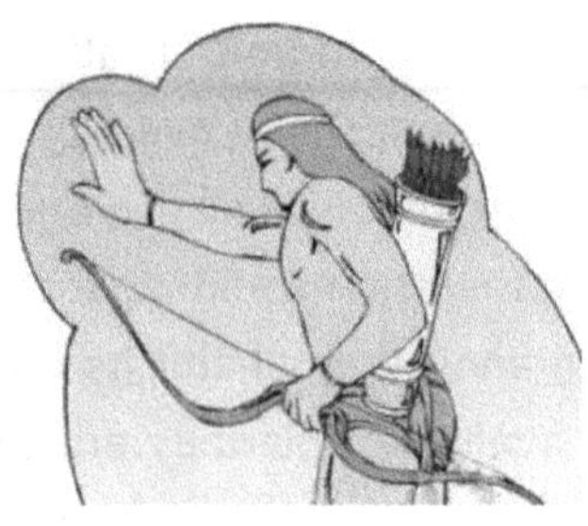

"Cowboys and Indians" are a classic pair in conflict. The subject they fight over could be "wilderness". The Indian's goal could be "to be respectful of the wilderness". The cowboy's could be

"to dominate the wilderness". Each side is made solid by all kinds of fixed ideas, experiences, confrontations, etc. They are both "right extreme" in their traditional identities.

The Theme

The general subject matter of a GPM is called the theme. In Ron Hubbard's materials it is known as the End-word. The most basic themes on a case are broad general concepts that can cover a lot of situations and territory. It could be "wealth", "survival", "eternity", "consciousness", "faith", "health", "beauty", "justice", "serenity", etc., etc. They cover broad concepts that have been important to living for millions of years. These core themes sound like philosophical areas of interest that people can feel passionate about. They are "Absolutes". Yet "Absolutes are unobtainable" and therefore never completed as goals. They can, however, be dealt with as highly charged subjects. You will usually start out with more tangible themes related to daily life. They may derive much of their force from deeper, older basic themes to which they are related. Themes, over vast spans of time, tend to repeat themselves and thus reappear in a cyclical pattern. This is known as the Downward Spiral. The theme re-appears, but now smaller in scope, as there is a loss of power due to the fact that more and more attention units get tied up in old goals, identities and mental masses. It is, however, important to note that to work out "whole-track charts" and Line Plots aren't part of the presented technology. To try to map them outside research serves no good purpose. They will reveal themselves when the client is ready. Feel free to find them piece by piece as results of cognitions.

Whatever the person brings up as a hot theme can usually be run as long as it is in a "timeless and qualitative" form. By "timeless" we mean in a form that can be found independent of any particular time and place. By "qualitative" we mean, it at its core has a quality, flavor or "feel" to it rather than being a thing. "The theme of law" would cover anything related to law matters which all belong to one GPM. The example could include anything related to the police force, to courts, to lawbreakers, crime, loot, victims, etc. Despite this diversity, all elements in this GPM would have a certain "feel", flavor or quality in common. A theme is such a broad category characterized by a common quality, "feel" or flavor. This abstract quality is what holds the GPM together in the mind.

The basic conflicts we go through in life may change in personnel and circumstances. Yet, the emotions and drama patterns are stunningly similar anywhere on the time track. A hot theme is something that engages and appeals to the person. It's something the person expends effort on, agonizes over. It could be something that ruins his life and consumes his attention, interest and energy. Any area that continuously causes out rudiments on a case is a strong indicator of a theme that can be processed once its "timeless and qualitative" form is formulated. Initially it could be the job, the boss, the spouse or kids, how one looks, one's special nemesis, the tax man, etc.

If we take the theme "wealth" as example, you can see how many conflicts and wars that theme has led to going way back in time. How many goals and counter goals have gone into that theme! Examples would be "to create wealth", "to gather wealth", "to protect wealth", "to retain wealth", "to steal wealth", "to pretend wealth", "to ridicule wealth", "to avoid wealth", "to destroy wealth". The examples show the deterioration of ambition to a point where the last one "to destroy wealth" is the opposite of the first one, "to create wealth". At the very end the person has, typically, switched sides and become what he was fighting so hard when he first set out "to create wealth". Such destructive goals are usually of short duration as it's against the basic goodness of a Being. An up-scale goal, such as "to create wealth" is usually the first and most basic goal in a GPM ("create" is the top level of the Havingness Scale). The opposing goal to any given goal is not necessarily its logical opposite. It is simply the counter-goal that completely frustrated the person and caused him to give up the original activity. Counter-goals to "to create wealth" could be, "to scatter wealth", "to tax wealth", "to detest wealth", and of course, "to destroy wealth". Once the most basic goal (and its opposition) is discharged, the whole GPM is erased. The most basic goal the person pursued in a GPM would be the original unopposed intention just to postulate something into existence. This may be found, and usually may not, the first time the theme is contacted and available goals run. Often general unburdening of charge is needed on a number of themes before the earliest pair of goals of any given GPM is unburdened enough to produce a read on the meter so they can be run.

Since a person, as he exists in present time, has countless GPMs as part of his case, chances are that many different ones are affecting him. After all, each GPM consists of long sections of his time track organized according to theme, goals and polarity. Sections of a GPM can go in and out of restimulation depending on the person's intentions, activities and environment in present time. This is, in other words, a very complex and confusing situation we are dealing with.

Unburdening The GPM Case

In the original research of Hubbard, it was considered necessary to uncover one Actual GPM in its entirety, following the internal pattern called the Line Plot. Various researchers in the Freezone have found this impractical to do or too hard on the person. Instead, one can view a person's case as a complexity of intermingled GPMs that has to be taken apart from the top down, so to speak. You want to remove the dichotomies you can get to without stirring up additional charge. You keep this up, taking the most available dichotomies and once that one is removed, you look for the next available one and keep it up until done. You unburden the case gently rather than insisting on a theoretical form that undoubtedly exists below or inside the mess. The truth is, to tear down an old structure (such as an old building) it is not necessary to know all the details about how it was built and operated. Instead, you make a careful plan and blow up the key pillars -- or you simply bulldoze the whole area flat.

To tear down an old structure--be it a building or a mental structure as a GPM--it is not necessary to know exactly how it was built and how it operated. One simply needs to know some solid basic principles so it is possible to unsettle the structure and it will collapse. Ron Hubbard actually used this principle in other parts of processing. He talked about locating the linchpins and pulling those out and the aberrated mechanism and condition would collapse.

Another thing that makes this approach unique, compared to Hubbard's GPM techniques, is the care taken in discharging not only the goals but also the identities (IDs) behind each goal. Each ID came about as the Beingness assumed in order to effectively pursue a goal. A goal like, "to enforce the law", makes you think of a police man–and that is the typical ID related to that goal. Each of these IDs hardened while pursuing its goal. It adopted fixed ideas, survival strategies, lies, etc. in an attempt to remain a force focused on succeeding. A goal is, in other words, not seen as a mathematical vector in an abstract universe but as a chapter in one's personal history book. It headlines personal battles, victories and defeats, tenacity, cruelty and underhanded practices used in the battle in order to prevail. Often you find your own past ID in a certain conflict is now hopelessly intermingled with "the enemy's" ID. This intermingling of IDs is part of what makes it persist as mental mass formed around the dormant but "not dead yet" opposing goals of the conflict. To take the mess apart completely, you have to look at the IDs of the combatants, including their fixed ideas, etc. These ideas, etc. solidified the IDs opposing "just causes" to a point where they to this day are worth fighting for when restimulated. The identities and the fixed ideas that hold them in place are the most basic "lies" in the GPMs. A Being can be anything. In the context of the GPM he passionately decided to be, say, a police man and made sure to be a "damned good cop" by adopting all kinds of fixed ideas and justifications. This is a long way from his natural potential. It's a huge alter-is or "lie" that keeps the person being solid and aberrated. It is, however, also a way to give the goal pursued persistence and power.

The top-down approach means that you not necessarily get the very first time a goal was conceived. You may take up subjects that are less than at the very core of the case. Likewise, you don't necessarily get the earliest incidents when the goal was in play. Sometimes you get high-powered copies. But you are unburdening the case and your ability to spot earlier occurrences and more basic themes will improve as you continue. Just take what comes to you and run that and leave it at that. You flatten a goal by repeating it and acknowledging each repetition. You keep up using Repeater Technique until it no longer produces a change or read. Both when finding themes and goals you should go with the first answer that pops up in your mind. (Sometimes you may have to rework the formulation to run it.) The technique is known as "Flash Answers". The mechanism is also known as the mind's File Clerk. Once you have found a hot theme, you stay with that theme until you can find no more charged goals connected with it. A goal always has the form "to [verb] theme". See examples above related to wealth.

Completing GPMs

Actual GPMs in their entirety may not be available at first contact, as mentioned above. You may only be able to find and run a few pairs before something more urgent demands to be run. To get it all, it is therefore important to go back and recheck themes from time to time. This should at least be given great care before finishing the whole action. A GPM is erased when its first pair is dealt with. The very first item in the GPM is the person's original postulated goal related to that theme. Erasing this will usually result in a significant blowdown and wide floating needle on an e-meter. The cycle has finally been "completed" by undoing the stuck postulate. The first goal in a GPM will be an upscale "free spirit" postulate, such as "to create [theme]". Different systems can be developed to find as many themes as possible. You can ask to specific spheres of life for instance. We have found that asking for what a person is dramatizing (the main question used in the process R-6-EW) may yield additional themes that then can be taken through the Goals-ID steps. Since finding live and important themes requires that the person can look at his life "objectively" or with self-critique, the action requires that the person is in good shape and has completed grades 0-4 and Dianetics (grade 5). This is also why the rundown works best as a duo-action rather than a solo action. We have often found that great themes come to mind in some odd life situation or as a result of reading and works when checked out in session. There are, of course, also more formalized ways to find hot themes.

Rounding off

In the light of the tremendous case gains that can be gotten from finding and running the polarities of Actual GPMs, it is a mystery how this whole band of technical possibilities got so utterly abandoned. Many old-timers, from the 1961-65 period, assumed it would be taken up on the advanced OT levels. This with good reason as it was placed as the top level of the 1965 grade chart. What we have from Ron Hubbard now seems, however, to be all about attached entities (bodyless spirits attached to the person's body9) as they are processed in various ways On the advanced levels. Using the approach of the Goals-ID Rundown you will realize that there is plenty to take up from the experiential track. When you embark on this action, you will experience a profound positive effect on your ability to be, do and have in daily life in the form of stable gains.

Chapter 9: GPM Series 3
Games and GPMs

It is said, what makes organic life in this universe tick is the urge to survive and thrive. To make it worthwhile to spiritual Beings, however, there must be fun and games. So having a game is right up there--and Survival itself could be understood as a game. We as Beings love games. Above all, it seems, there must be a game–and that's where the trouble starts...

According to one definition a game consists of freedoms, barriers and purposes.

You can have simple games where you don't really have opponents. An artist can simply go out in nature, set up his scaffold and paint a picture of what he sees. His immediate purpose is to paint a pretty picture; his ultimate goal: to create Beauty. The barriers are all the difficulties that have to be overcome in order to put it on a canvas. The freedoms are the many practical and artistic choices to be made before he is done.

When we talk about games we do, however, normally talk about two sides competing against each other; or about a number of competitors competing against other participants, such as in a race. Besides freedoms, barriers and purposes, we here find opposition in the form of opponents or competitors.

A game usually has opponents and something the participants fight over. In soccer we have two opposing teams fighting over control of the ball in order to score on the opponent.

When we talk about a *games-condition* we here mean a certain state of mind where the player or players have become obsessed with a game and can't take their attention off it. You could initially think of an obsessive gambler who has moved well beyond a healthy state of mind. He keeps gambling because he is hooked. His eyes hang onto the roulette and he is afraid to look the other way, even for a second. In games-conditions we typically have two opponents obsessed with fighting each other. It's often an "I love to hate..." type of situation. Examples of games-conditions would be the Cold War, the Israeli-Palestinian conflict or a divorced couple that always finds something to fight about, be it custody of children, visitation arrangements or their common furniture and things. They are in it for the fight. Once one problem is solved a new problem is instantly found and endlessly exploited. Their family life has decayed into a family feud.

The Goals Problems Mass

A GPM is a super problem of sorts that has layers and mental mass to it. There are numerous GPMs stored in a person's mind. Each GPM is a collection of old conflicts and games-conditions. The basic elements of a GPM are: a goal and the identity pursuing the goal (self in some form); a counter-goal and the identity behind it (the opponent). Such a pair is called a dichotomy or polarity. A GPM, furthermore, contains a series of such similar dichotomies, one layered on top of the previous one. These conflicts are all held together by a common subject matter or theme. Big examples of GPMs in action are, as mentioned, the Cold War (theme: world supremacy); the Middle East conflict (theme: the land of Palestine) or a stormy marriage headed for divorce (theme: marriage). The problems and conflicts in one GPM are all related as they are fights over the same subject matter, the same theme. Both sides want to win the game they are playing, be it in politics, war or in life. The super-problem of the GPM in play is constantly being added to and made even harder to resolve as these kinds of conflicts are intimate parts of living and surviving. GPMs do, however, also exist as completed matters on the track. At some point the game is declared ended. The local convenience store owner may at some point on his track have been a player in the game of "world supremacy". It hasn't bothered him much lately. He gave up on that theme eons ago. Once one walks away from a theme completely the GPM is "ended" or simply stored on the track as part of one's history. Yet, even in this case it can be restimulated and come back into play; say, when the store owner plans for supremacy in the local convenience store market. A GPM, in other words, contains a wealth of experience and patterns on how to react to things and handle opposition related to its theme. It's a recipe for how to be, do and have in that regard.

The Line Plot

The GPM gets initially formed step by step as the person lives through the eons. One conflict comes to an end and gets layered as sediments and fossils at the bottom of the sea. This happens when the person stops pursuing a certain goal and modifies it. A new conflict based on the modified goal on the same theme comes into play, only to be layered on top of the previous one in due time. It starts with a big idea and no thought of opposition. Just like the artist above who wanted to create Beauty. Over time, he may have to modify his goal time and again to stay in the art game. The goal will step by step degrade to less ambitious ones due to the opposition. From being the postulate of a free spirit it eventually becomes that of a trodden down player that, despite all, still has a passion for art and beauty. From his original dream of being the greatest artist who ever lived he has become a shy assistant in an art store sweeping the floors.

Below is a fictive example related to a woman's marriage. It shall be noted that the "Marriage GPM" is not a record of one marriage with its ups and downs. It's a composite of the woman's whole track marriage history as it's grouped in her mind. It will thus include many different identities, periods and scenarios on both sides of the dichotomies. Yet, the woman has this blueprint that very well may determine the fate of her current marriage. It shall be noted that goals and identities have to be found individually for each person to have any value.

Note: This article is about Actual GPMs. In Implant GPMs the goals follow the exact same pattern and wording from person to person. An example is OT-2 that is run using printed lists of implanted goals. These set goal-series were implanted as a type of "brain washing" in the distant past. As a citizen, we assume, you went into a clinic and got "brain washed" by electronic means. All citizens, one could theorize, had to receive this treatment to remain in good standing. The effectiveness of these Implant GPMs rested on the fact that the person had Actual GPMs that were restimulated.

The below is thus only meant as an illustration:

Identity	Goal		Opposing Goal	Opposing Identity
Woman in love	to create the perfect marriage	–><–	to break up the future marriage	Future mother-in-law
Wife in love	to establish the perfect marriage	–><–	to cast doubt in the perfect marriage	Woman's old friends
Realistic wife	to sustain a good marriage	–><–	to "supplement" the marriage	Cheating husband
Angry wife	to defend a challenged marriage	–><–	to ignore a good marriage	Army recruiter
Troubled wife	to scrutinize the marriage	–><–	to sabotage the marriage	Drinking husband
Resigned wife	to pretend a good marriage	–><–	to "test" the marriage	Potential lover
Furious wife	to break up the marriage	–><–	to try to save the marriage	Amendful husband

As you can see, countless movie scripts could be built over this GPM. When you hear people "are playing games" with each other, you often find they are operating on old goals and identities that don't serve anyone's interest. They are dramatizing their GPM cases. Also note, the original opposition goal was "to break up the marriage". As the GPM came to an end it briefly became the wife's own goal. This is the sad proof of the maxim "What you resist you become" and also why it's such a good idea to get one's GPM case handled. Add to the example above that the wife's husband has his own GPM case related to marriage that can look and play out quite differently from hers and you will know why marriages can be troubled. There is another thing to note about the series of goals in the example. Each goal runs on a cycle of action. It starts with the intention to succeed doing the goal. The opposition will, at some point, make the person give up on it and decide on a change of tactics, which is the next goal down in the Line Plot. The succession of goals runs likewise on a cycle of action until "to break up the marriage" ends it all. The original Line Plot of a basic GPM is formed in chronological order. The pattern of goals is, however, repeated many times on the time track and often out of the original sequence. As it exists in the present it can best be described as a sorting system that sorts experiences and efforts related to the theme. The GPMs could be said to float in time. They are in part being used as a portable reference library each time the person meets a challenging situation. The person has this library of ready-made responses whether they fit the situation or not. It's a well known observation that "history repeats itself", be it in marriage or politics. Each time a new marriage or era is begun, it starts with high hopes and high in the Line Plot. All possibilities are open. As things develop, more incidents and charge are added to the already existing goals pursued earlier. The identities behind them become more and more mired into fixed ideas and set expectations. You see the whole spectrum play out when young and visionary people rebel against the establishment run by solid citizens.

The Goals

Let's take a step back and look at goals more philosophically. They are the reason the GPMs formed in the first place. You begin with a free Being to whom all possibilities are open. He is, however, bored. So he decides it's time for some action. He decides on something to do -- on a goal. The basic goals on a case are lofty concepts, be it "to fight for justice", "to create beauty", "to facilitate understanding", etc. No matter how lofty a goal may be, deciding on one is an action of exclusion and individuation. Once you "fight for justice" countless other possibilities are excluded. There are many activities you can't participate in, such as simply having a good time as you constantly have to worry about what's going on around you. And fighting for justice will get you enemies. In other words, once you settle on a goal you have a "me and them" situation; you have created a split and a polarity that will generate charge. In order to generate power, each pole in this polarity has to be able to persist and hold its position. To accomplish this an identity is formed. It is modeled to serve the goal and be an anchor for that goal. This gives the goal persistence and the capability to generate power. Yesterday's power plant is, however sadly, today's reactive charge generator that can make life very unpleasant.

The good thing about goals is, once you have decided on one you have a game. You have a better chance at achieving happiness, as happiness can be defined as pursuing a goal successfully and eventually accomplishing it. Also, goals are so important to living that people without goals are considered bums. Once you pursue a goal, you have a role to play in life, you are part of existence. There is a distinct role, identity or character connected with a certain well-defined goal. It's a whole package of characteristics, knowledge, experience and agreements. The reason for this identity, is to be what one has to be in order to succeed.

There is another characteristic about goals that is crucial to the forming of GPMs. That is the fact that old goals don't necessarily just fade away and disappear. This is partly because they have been anchored in solid identities. More importantly, some goals are so basic that they always are part of existence, even when not pursued actively. It also seems to be a characteristic of Beings that they never totally give up on old goals.

Basic goals include "to create beauty" and the many other goals that are part of the games of being human and a spiritual Being in this universe. Other goals you find in a GPM are typically abandoned goals, but they failed and their cycle never completed. They still exist as dormant intentions. Unless one at some point decided to undo the goal completely by deconstructing it and its anchor, it will still exist in a dormant form that can be revived as a dramatization.

A GPM, thus, could be said to be a collection of successive own incomplete goals that have accumulated charge. Each goal is anchored in an identity. The charge-mechanism of the GPM has become permanent as the goals, one by one, are hung up against the anchored opposition goals that made them fail. The effort or resistance each side executed towards the other side, and still executes when restimulated, builds up charge and mass. All goals and identities in one particular GPM are held together by a common theme.

Being Tough and Determined

To survive in this universe one has to be tough and determined. As Ron Hubbard said, "Only the tigers survive, and they have a hard time too". To succeed with a goal one has to be of a single mind.

This has to be expressed and anchored in one's beingness to work and be recognized by others. The toughness is ensured by opinions, agreements and fixed ideas held by the individual. All this, combined with professional knowledge, forms the identity behind the goal. In any war, soldiers are taught to see the enemy as totally evil and inhuman. They are told it's a just war and God is on their side. Only in this manner can they keep fighting and killing. A whole army culture of fixed ideas, altered facts and lies will blossom. These fixed ideas, being "lies", make the identity of, say, being a "God's soldier" persist, even after the war is long over. Once a person in processing is made to find a number of these fixed ideas related to the past identity of a "God's soldier", he can undo that old identity. Needless to say, numerous past identities are highly irrational in the person's present environment.

Each profession and occupation has its own professional beingness a member of that occupation has to adhere to. Be it a doctor, a priest, a cowboy, or a ballerina. There is a whole set of skills and agreements that goes with each occupation.

The toughness, skill set and single-mindedness that go with a role in life is essential to successfully practice a profession or play a game. One has to be recognized as, say, a doctor in order to do healing work and get a respectable job. To gain the proper recognition one may have to adapt many inexplicable habits, characteristics, opinions and points of view–their origin often lost in history.

When it comes to past games and GPMs, these solid identities (valences or characters) are part of what is wrong with the person. The goals in the GPMs are anchored by identities and the identities are anchored by fixed ideas and old agreements. It is not enough to simply find the goals and bleed some charge off them. The "tough" identities, that are the poles that perpetuate the generation of charge, have to be found as well and the fixed ideas they operated on have to be inspected thoroughly before the whole thing can be taken apart for real. Once this is done, you will typically see the two identities or poles melt and sort of reconcile with one another. What's actually happening is, they have been dis-created as somewhat autonomic fixtures in the mind. The goals and identities in the dichotomy have been resolved. The person being processed has gained a new ability to see it from both these two characters' points of view and has thus obtained a new wholeness, a new and higer level of pan-determinism.

Processing GPMs

If it only were a matter of finding the goals the whole thing would long ago have been resolved. It seems to me, what made Ron Hubbard's GPM research of the early 1960s come out short of effective standard processes, was the fact that it was focused on mapping the whole structure of the GPMs. It was, as research, a pursuit to find the Line Plots and the sequence the themes would line themselves up in on the time line of existence. The GPMs were found to be packages containing all the better known reactive elements, such as traumas, losses, problems, misdeeds/secrets, upsets, fixed ideas and special identities (characters). All phenomena, associated with a certain theme, would group themselves into this mega-structure known as the GPM. This mix of aberrative content is, of course, already being contacted on the grades and what can be confronted is being addressed. *What the more recent research of GPMs has shown is, there is much left of the GPM core structures that has hardly been touched. This is well worth pursuing as "the GPMs imitate life" as well as "life imitates the GPMs".* They are formed as records of the games of life we have been involved in since the beginning of time and are the cause of "history repeating itself". The instructions, role models and patterns they contain are followed or fought against repeatedly, over and over, more or less reactively. When processing the GPMs, the person is being re-introduced to old endeavors, to old friends and foes and all the good and hard times he had during these undertakings, people and identities in the past.

When you take a case apart on the level of GPMs, you will find whole new aspects not really touched anywhere else in processing. It is important to do it right. You have to approach the task in a very disciplined way. The most important rule in modern GPM processing is to discharge the contacted goals and identities thoroughly before doing anything else. This includes handling any present time upsets, problems and fixed ideas the identities may have inside the dichotomy. The approach is one step at the time and confronting clear and present danger rather than trying to jump ahead and solve the whole riddle. You are walking through a booby-trapped terrain that requires all your attention and presence of mind while dealing with it. You have to remove each booby trap methodically and not try to rush things forward.

It has been found, what you run into of restimulation on any given person's GPM case is a scramble of dichotomies from many different GPMs. They were formed at very different times of the person's time-track. Their goals and identities are now part of the reactive experience the person is operating on. Rather than working out a research map you have to follow the very basics of processing used at the lower end of the Bridge. You have to destimulate and discharge what's there before you trigger and restimulate new charge. You have to parallel what the mind is doing. You have to deal with what the person's attention is stuck on and can confront.

Note: This may sound like Routine-6 (R6-End-Words) to oldtimers. The real difference is that goals and identities are completely discharged and deconstructed when running GPMs by themes. In R6-EW triggered and restimulated goals are taken to a win only without trying to find identities or exhaust themes. R6-EW was released in 1965 where there was a great need to remove the charge that research students had run into during experimental GPM processing and the process was well suited for that. It seems less relevant when you start from a clean slate.

Modern GPM running by themes takes all this into account. You start out finding a hot theme. It's an area of the person's life he/she has trouble with, is concerned about and active in. In short, it's an area of ongoing drama in the person's life. There are, of course, numerous themes in play in any given person at any given time. It reflects the many areas and subjects that make up life. Once a hot theme is established, you find a charged goal belonging to that theme. You take some charge off it. You find the opposing goal and take some charge off that. You then find the identity behind each goal. You bleed each goal for remaining charge, then bleed the identities for charge by finding the fixed ideas, lies and out rudiments they are sitting in. *All these factors anchor the identities, that anchor the goals, that anchor the GPM structure.*

The goal forms the identity. The identity is held in place by fixed ideas, including cultural and educational ones. Of special interest are arbitrary ideas of own rightness and superiority.

A persistent identity is found to hold on to these beyond reason in a determined and ornery way to prove self right and others wrong. Since the identity has its attention on its goal and opposition, rather than self, the fixed ideas remain unseen and un-inspected.

***Butler's goal:** "to serve nobility". Fixed ideas could be: "a real butler shows no emotion"*

"I am the best", "I am more worthy than them", "they are decadent and childish", etc.

In processing GPMs effectively, you pay no attention to the Line Plot. There are too many themes in play to concentrate on just one GPM. As the person progresses well in this processing, the Line Plots will reveal themselves at some point and can now possibly be tracked down theme for theme, GPM for GPM. Still, it is like Dianetics, where it's more important to find the body sensations (somatic) and then the related incidents the person can confront and process those, rather than trying to find Basic Basic in the first session. (The sensation as an item could be compared to the special flavor of the theme found in GPM processing. The somatic holds a Dianetics chain together as the theme with its special flavor holds the GPM together.) So you process the dichotomies you can get without forcing the issue. You make a note and recheck the theme later in order to complete themes.

It's a matter of unburdening the case by taking up charge that offers itself to be run next. Done this way, you bring about optimum progress and an amazing amount of case change per session. Furthermore, since it's all based on the person's ability to confront and there will be things to run whether one is a retired house wife or leader of an army, there is no particular reason to wait until the person is way up the advanced levels. It can be delivered after grade 4, after Dianetics or after OT-3. It can be done once the person is in good shape. It works well once the person has gotten rid of the charge processed on the grades on the grades and has developed the perceptions necessary to run the GPM procedures.

Games and Games-Conditions are an intimate part of life. They lead to all kinds of aberrative incidents. The way it all stacks up on a case over the millennia is what is described as the GPMs. Modern GPM processing is a safe way to undo the damage of lost games, of freeing a person of living through the same mistakes and disasters over and over. It frees up the person to, again, be, do and have without dramatizations.

Chapter 10: GPM Series 4

GPMs: Adventurous Routine 2-12

A Study in the 1960s GPM Tech

Routine 2-12 was intended as a beginning level process for handling Actual GPMs. It was introduced at Saint Hill in England in November of 1962. It held a lot of promise and led to gains of great magnitude. It was, however, not possible at the time to find an approach that could be executed uniformly by auditors; nor was it that all clients could run the process. Consequently R2-12 led to several disasters. Untimely death and insanity are reported as the grim "side effects" of running the program inexpertly in the field. This article is based on reviewing relevant lectures and writings from 1962-63 and from first-hand accounts found in internet newsgroups and elsewhere. My hope is that the article is understandable to readers not trained in tech.

In the Technical Volumes you will, under the date of 23 November, 1962, find the principal bulletin that covers the process R2-12. It begins this way: "This Procedure is to be done on every HGC client, every course student of every course as a client, as early as possible.... Done correctly it will end the no-results or slow result case and guarantee faster gain to the fast case. ALL Cases must have this done at once."

The Rationale of R2-12

The idea of the process is to handle long term problems that the client is sitting in. The apparently biggest problem of all, is when the client in present time is opposed by persons or identities he perceives as hostile or antagonistic to him. If this sounds familiar to today's Scientologists it is no accident. That cases wouldn't advance in the presence of major problems had been known since the 1950s. After the short reign of R2-12, the same datum of "cases won't advance in the presence of major present time problems" became an intricate part of handling suppression and feeling suppressed. According to the tech, the handling of major problem-relationships is priority number one. But usually "the problem" is identified by proving "the other guy" completely wrong and designate him/her a suppressive person. This oftentimes has puzzled people and caused them to reject the PTS tech. Truth told, it is an over-simplification of what is going on as only one side of the problem is taken into account.

The theory of R2-12, it seems, is more to the point. It clearly addresses the client as the other, and often hidden, side of the problem. This theory is more factual, although it may not be a truth all clients are ready for. R2-12 addressed both sides of the problem. It takes two to tango; it takes a clash of personalities to create a problem of magnitude as a problem is intention versus counter-intention; goal versus counter-goal; or identity versus counter-identity. What R2-12 sought to handle, was to fully identify the two identities in conflict and have them discharge against each other in session. In a lecture called "R2-12, Theory and Practice II" (lecture SHSBC 621129) Ron covers the basics. Here is his explanation of how it relates to GPMs:

"Now, why is it called...a Goals Problem Mass? It is a mass which is composed of identities which oppose identities. And they are so delicately faced against each other on the track that they don't slip. They're right there and they finally compose a great big, gaudy, black mass."

Also, the R2-12 bulletin says: "The Goals Problem Mass consists of Items (identities, valences) in opposition to one another. Any pair of these Items, in opposition to each other, constitutes a specific problem."

In other words, the perceived suppressive person comprises the one side of the problem and is corresponding to a valence, identity or so-called Reliable Item in the client's mind. Opposed to that is the client's own perceived identity. It is, in principle, a very old conflict that has been restimulated by present circumstances. Ron goes on giving an example where a person in the valence of an arsonist is clashing with The National Insurance Company:

"If this fellow has his attention, his overtness, fixated on any present time thing, then we assume that that present time thing represents a piece of the GPM. And that, hidden and out of sight, is its opposing piece. This person never asks himself, 'Who or what would oppose the National Insurance Company?' That he never asks, because in the first place he is Joe Jones and he is opposing the National Insurance Company and he has keyed in the terminal (identity) 'arsonist' and the opposition terminal (identity) is 'insurers'. See, it's a nice game and it's buried right there in the GPM. But this thing is so keyed in in present time that this individual is being audited continuously with a present time problem. In session he always, some part of some session, his thinkingness will fixate on the National Insurance Company. He'll compare all this as to how it relates to the National Insurance Company. He will want to get well so that he can be powerful enough to blow the top of the building off. All of his auditing is being coned in toward this. In other words, his fixation on present time is such that he never goes backtrack. He's trying to audit himself up to something or other. In other words, he's dramatizing the companion dumbbell, see? The other ball there that is opposing that thing, 'insurers'. Now, the National Insurance Company is not part of the bank. It is a key-in. It is a substitute for, a lock on, this GPM thing that keeps it in continuous restimulation."

The Dumbbell is a graphic illustration of the two sides in opposition that make up a dichotomy in the GPM. It also illustrates the equal size and strength of the opposed identities that is needed for the GPM to remain an equilibrium of forces.

In the quote we have: Opposition terminal: Insurer.
Own terminal: Arsonist;
two natural enemies that are combating each other.

In other words, R2-12 gives the underlying reason why some persons have a deeply suppressive effect on a certain case while other apparently equally bad persons have little or no effect on the same case – as the client simply can brush the latter ones off. It all comes down to the identity the client is operating from and the goal he reactively is pursuing. In modern PTS handling, the things that R2-12 attacks head on, are gently taken to a degree of release and the client is instructed to stay away from the suppressive terminal as he/she walks around in the flesh. But this key-out handling misses an important point and tends to make clients see themselves as innocent victims. It's a limited tech.

Auditing R2-12

The process was a Routine 2 process because it was designated to be done by Class II auditors at the time. It had 12 steps and thus it was R2-12. In contrast to R3 processes (intended for class 3 auditors) the procedure did not look for the major goals behind GPMs that outline the games and wars going on inside the GPM and is the basis around which the whole GPM is built. One only looked for opposition terminals (identities) in present time and matched them up with own terminals. Once these were matched up, the process was complete. Nothing was done in session to further discharge the pair.

As mentioned, R2-12 is one of the roughest processes that you can find in the Technical Volumes. Don't try to run it at home. Years later, you would meet old timers that proudly would brag "I was audited on 2-12 and I survived!" It was seen as a badge of honor and proof of toughness to have gone through that. How come the process was so rough? A good part of the explanation lies in that auditing at the time only was partly codified. Things that auditors later got to respect as basic laws when it came to programming and doing actions, such as listing, were lessons Ron learned the hard way from research auditing, including R2-12. In other words, the way R2-12 was executed was in blatant violation of the C/S Series technical bulletins of the 1970s and of Laws of Listing and Nulling of 1968.

The full title of the technical bulletin also gives a clue: "R2-12. Opening Procedure by Rock Slam." The thing the auditor was primarily looking for was a rock slamming identity (an evil or ill-intended character that shows up on an e-meter as an irregular and wild dance of a needle). And once a rock slamming opposition was found, one would look for a rock slamming valence the client occupied. The significance of the rock slam is today "evil purpose" or area or character of extreme destructive nature. In 1962 rock slams were (correctly) seen as the extreme games-condition that would exist on the two sides of the dichotomy. It was the hallmark indicator of the war zone that exists between the terminal and opposition terminal. There was little thought of the havoc that was stirred up by assessing for the war zone. Once the rock slams were turned on, the process was complete; "the client could be sent to home – the action was complete.

A dichotomy in a GPM typically consists of two identities that are natural enemies.

In looking for rock slamming identities, the auditor tried to locate two terminals in an extreme games-condition -- enemies that were at each others' throats. The client may have a long history being one of them and opposing the other. Oftentimes, the client has been occupying both identities at different points of his whole timeline history.

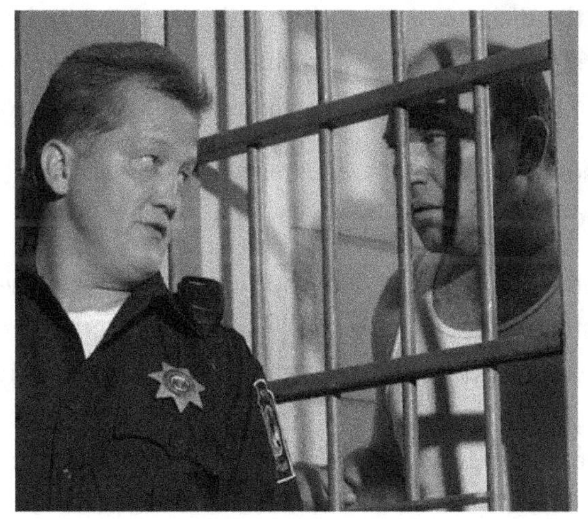

Also, the main way identities were discharged in R2-12 was through making long lists. The idea was, once the client was listing, locks would be peeled off the core item, the core valence the client was either occupying or opposing. The bulletin furthermore states: "Complete the list as in any listing. Don't stop just because the client protested or wept." Apparently, the Listing done on R2-12 could be a brutal affair of "forcing the client". Doing listing like that today, is obviously a "no no" and a "technical high crime" according to standard tech rules. In hindsight from the Laws of Listing and Nulling (1968) this was an endless action of overlisting by forcing the client. It was prone to restimulate all kinds of other things in the bank. Other identities, other conflicts, other GPMs.

Alan C. Walter, who was a research auditor in the 1960s, put it this way in an internet newsgroup (ACT 2002):

"The reason [for the problems] was the way listing and nulling was done. In those days we listed deep and long. It was nothing to list 2 or 3,000 item lists. And this was long before any form of correction lists. Only the fittest survived."

Following the Laws of Listing and Nulling of 1968, an auditor usually finds the right item on a list within 10 items. Going beyond finding the item is considered an error, an overrun.

In 1962, according to the quote above, lists with thousands of items were not uncommon. It wasn't seen as out tech but as a way to discharge and establish the Reliable Items, the core identities at war. Some auditors that didn't follow these, in hindsight, horrifying instructions to the letter actually had better success. Listen to this story by "Huggie". "Huggie" is the screen name of an old time field auditor from New Zealand. His initial experience with R2-12 was posted to news group ACT in 2002:

"I was a field auditor about 500 miles from the HASI (nearest organization). I had to get it right or starve. I had just about reached 'burn out' from listening to all the messy muck of clients lives, and sometimes helping them see it in a more causative light, but often just stuck to Hell and unable to see where it had gone wrong.

"I loved it when R2-12 came out. Now, I didn't have to trace up those jungles of sh*t anymore and listen to them indefinitely. Just get the item, terminal and balance the oppositions. (That's getting into the dichotomies which rule this world). I had nobody to tell me not to evaluate a wrong item. I wasn't going to tolerate a rising, dirty needle when I figured that I must have done something wrong in the last minute or so. You didn't have to have a rocket scientist's brain to figure that out.

"I had a BALL with it. I called in one failed client after another and between October and February I made enough money to go to Saint Hill.

When I got there, I was shocked to find they were not doing R2-12 anymore. When I started boasting about it, everybody told me about their failures and 'don't you know it ploughed in everyone who has run it; so you better stuff up.' Hell I was just ignorant I had NOBODY to tell me how BAD it was so I just ploughed on making good results and money. I looked at some of the students who had been bugged up by R2-12 and bit my lip to keep from betting them that I could have straightened it all out. But this was a good lesson in my first few days." Signed Huggie.

Apparently, Huggie could make R2-12 work and we can only guess how he diverted from the published version. Maybe he didn't overlist. Maybe he was more careful when he matched up antagonists. Maybe he simply let the client talk it out, discharging the restimulated case by letting the client talk freely about what he found.

Another client, audited on R2-12 by an expert auditor in California, had these less dramatic comments:

"I was audited on R2-12 and it wasn't bad. I got some charge off. But I had been running hot GPMs with R3M or some such process, and it seemed to me that R2-12 was a downgrade -- too shallow a gradient for me."

Huggie of New Zealand later had some very negative experiences with GPM auditing which he summarized this way in a blunt post to ACT:

"I have always said, 'the simpler the better.' You can stuff your complex GPMs which killed my lover and sent my best friend insane." (Apologies for the blunt language).

Obviously, this wasn't necessarily his own doing but what happened around him at the time. For obvious reasons, casualties and incidents like that were intolerable and resulted in R2-12 being discontinued after a few months. Around 1965 all research into Actual GPMs was discontinued as horror stories continued to accumulate. Instead, Implant GPMs were pursued where the auditor would have a fully mapped series of goals he could follow. Implants are incidents of overwhelm, usually by electronic means, where a long list of artificial goals would be "implanted" in the person's bank by an "implant crew". Implants tend to imitate actual GPMs but have not come about as a result of the client living his own goals and all his experiences and conflicts the goals led to. One can assume, all GPM research was abandoned after numerous incidents of high liability to Ron personally and to Scientology in general. It was, indeed, a group trauma of magnitude. Although these stories have been suppressed ever since, it makes the tragic death of Lisa McPherson in the mid 1990s seem bland.

The Power of GPMs

It seems obvious that the use of R2-12 and other GPM processes hit some high voltage on cases. It is charge of a magnitude we don't hear about today. According to a Ron Hubbard lecture "The client's own GPM has the power and velocity, over an implant GPM, of somewhere between a thousand or a hundred thousand to one" (SHSBC 630811).

In HCOB 9-28-63, Hubbard puts it this way: "The actual goals and items of the client are several thousand times more aberrative than Implant GPMs. It is almost amusing to note how hard Implanters work and what overts they run up, and to note as well that if it were not for a spiritual being's own Goals Problems Mass, they could effect nothing harmful. How hard they work. And all for nothing. They are not the source of aberration. They merely make the universe seem more unpleasant. As for creating aberration, they could not. Sleep lights, Screens, False picture projectors, Goal implants alike are wholly innocuous compared to the thetan's (spiritual being) own Goals Problems Masses. One aberrates himself. And if he did not, nobody else could. Anything worrying the client or reducing his capability or life potential is to be found in Actual Items or Goals, not in traumas (engrams) or implants. These are not primary causes. Only the client's own goals and items are capable of basically causing the trouble.

Obviously, it is worth taking a closer look at such areas and find out if there are safe ways to access and discharge this the GPM case. It seems the repercussions the research had on the group during the 1960s made everybody gun shy, including Ron. Ron never revisited the area but took another route of auditing implants and entities that seems a rather pale way of taking charge off the case by addressing other factors than the person's self-determined bad choices, postulates and aberrated games and wars going down the eons of his time-track.

R2-12 and Beyond

One reason why it's worth giving R2-12 another look, is that it is dealing with "clear and present danger". It does not deal in goals nor line plots. It deals with the GPMs' impact on daily life and relationships.

The rationale the process builds on can be used in conflict handlings, if not already done. Skilled conflict handlers can query to what the client does in order to bring about the antagonistic conflict. That is addressing the other side of the problem. One could also address the client's own beingness, say, by coaching the person's own conduct.

I don't see any technical problems with finding the two sides of the conflict situation, using modern Listing and Nulling skills. It may not be called for until existing tech has proven insufficient over time. It is a next level up. You find the opposition, the enemy, the Suppressive Person, the antagonist; then you find what beingness the client is in that is in opposition to that and you could discharge the two sides using modern processes, such as running confront and responsibility, etc.

At some point the client should be able to take responsibility for both sides of the conflict. Completely omitting looking at own side of such a conflict actually leads to games-conditions of its own. One could theorize that one reason Church of Scientology has become so combative and isolated is due to the one-sidedness of their conflict handlings. Also, since many freezoners have charge on the Church as it exists today, it may even be beneficial in some cases to treat the church as an opposition terminal and take it from there.

One thing that seems to have been learned by several researchers in the freezone, is that it's unwise to try to tackle the different layers of the GPM head on (the line plots) and all at once. There is real charge in the GPMs! High Voltage! Instead, one can deal with one conflict at the time, using this definition from the R2-12 bulletin: "The Goals Problem Mass consists of Items (valences, identities) in opposition to one another. Any pair of these Items, in opposition to each other, constitute a specific problem."

Using that definition, one can tackle a GPM by dealing with one well-defined problem at a time. That's the right gradient. Once one dichotomy is fully discharged, it's safe to look for the next related one. If one tries to follow the line plot right away, there are too many forks in the road to find one's way safely.

Conclusion

The discovery of the GPMs was an original discovery Ron made around 1961. In my opinion, it ranks with discoveries such as engrams (traumas containing recordings of pain and unconsciousness) and the grades. Actually, I rank it above that. The masses and significances in the mind, called the GPMs, are the compressed recordings of persistent conflicts the person went through and lost. They reflect what the person has been, done, and had since the beginning of time. When you begin to take these masses apart, you parallel (in reverse order) what the client has been doing for the duration of this universe and even before that. The discovery of the GPMs came out of processes addressing goals, like SOP Goals mentioned in the TRs bulletin. Goals were found to be red flags sticking up on a case. They led to major areas of conflict, charge and aberration. (Goals can still be used as a low end entry point to cases, by the way. There is a whole lost tech of using goals as entry points.) From auditing goals, the whole anatomy of GPMs was discovered piece by piece. Yet, the basics of the tech were not up to handling the charge encountered. In Alan Walter's words, "we were spiritual illiterates" during that research. "We couldn't handle the ascensions". In the pursuing years the research group of the original Saint Hill Special Briefing Course went through numerous traumatic incidents (such as blows, suicides, and serious illness). It eventually resulted in that the whole research was abandoned.

It is time to try to tackle the area with what we now know. I see GPMs as the real barrier to spiritual advancement; the next real barrier that is known. The conflicting goals and identities at war, the aberrated games they resulted in, are the elements that make up the GPMs. The answer to how and why we went down the dwindling spiral are found therein. Auditing the GPMs is to "parallel what the mind is doing" and has been doing for eons. Paralleling the client's mind is a basic rule for successful programming and auditing of cases. Today, we have the rules of standard tech as the basic rules you follow to get the best results with processes. We have "the laws of listing and nulling", we have "end phenomena of a process", etc., etc. From the C/S series technical bulletins we know the importance of set-ups and repairs. Taking all this into account makes it quite possible to develop the tech as it was intended. The downward spiral the GPM track describes is how we got less ambitious, less powerful and lost parts of ourselves. It is time to turn around and confront what happened and step by step take the long road back to our true beingness. That was my original dream when I came into Scientology and still is. Maybe it is yours too.

Chapter 11: GPM Series 5
GPMs and NOTs

(NOTs: Short for "New Era Dianetics for Operating Thetans" - an advanced processing level dealing with non-self energies called "entities" or "attachments" in mainstream spiritual teachings.) These "entities" are seen as originally live Beings but now in a miserable, frozen or "dead" state. They are also called BTs or Body Thetans. 'Thetan' is the Scientology word for spirit. An OT or Operating Thetan is someone who is operating at a high and very desirable cause level.

What we learned is that the theory of GPMs is relatively simple. After its discovery and early research in the 1960s however, the subject has been surrounded with considerable mysticism and warning signs due to its rocky history in Ron Hubbard's original research. On the 1965 edition of the grade chart, Actual GPMs were listed as the most advanced level. At the time, however, there was no approved technology to use to run it. Around 1967, what Ron called actual GPMs was completely dropped as part of the published grade chart. The general understanding from lectures and literature was that its place was above the published grade chart and it would be put back on the chart when the proper technology had been developed and tested. Instead, the published standard OT levels concentrated on implants, such as the original Clearing Course and OT-2, and on entities, such as OT-3 through OT-7.

Introduction of NOTs

In the very late 1970s, the Church of Scientology's OT levels were changed to include a heavy dose of NOTs auditing. OT-4 became the NOTs Drug Rundown, OT-5 audited NOTs and OT-6 and 7 were Solo NOTs.

NOTs -- or New Era Dianetics for Operating Thetans -- was first released in 1978 as a remedy for OTs who were having trouble running Dianetics. It was found that "entities" (body thetans and clusters of same), rather than the client himself, in many cases were the "individuals" holding the charge, holding the engrams. These disembodied spirits had to be addressed directly in order to handle that charge. Inexplicable pains, negative emotions and body conditions, that were usually considered the realm of engram running and Dianetics, were sometimes very troublesome to run on OTs. The "Dianetics" techniques (New Era Dianetics for OTs) of addressing the individual entities took care of much of that.

Soon thereafter, NOTs got extended to Solo NOTs (1979). It was claimed that completing these levels would lead to "cause over life". From being extracurricular rundowns, NOTs and Solo NOTs became part of the standard Bridge. One had to carry on until any and all "entities" within arms length were "blown". The Solo NOTs technique was designed to be a rather quick action (estimated to 25-50 hours) and an economical way of finishing the job of audited NOTs. That's how it was first announced by Hubbard. It soon got extended to be an almost endless action that, for many, took over a decade to complete. The tech assumes that the client has no more case of his own, no more time track. All there is left to do is the handling of these entities all around him. The entities are seen as the cause of all his ills and shortfalls. After getting rid of their influence, however, the client is considered completely caseless and ready for the "real OT levels" that consist of drills of OT abilities. The Solo NOTs tech is a 'clean-out of entities' action as none of the client's own problems and aberrations are directly addressed. The tech focuses all on structure — the entities — rather than function — the client's own postulates, goals, purposes, fixed ideas and aberrations as they came about and stuck over the eons of existence in this universe.

Good for Business

We have found that Solo NOTs has been considerably overextended from its original definition and concept of handling body conditions on OTs after they shouldn't run Dianetics anymore. This overextension coincided with Ron Hubbard's retirement from the scene and the new management's take-over. One could suspect more attention was paid to the business side of things and less attention given to the technical validity as long as it brought in new customers and business. In hindsight "cause over life" seems a great selling point but nothing more. Addressing entities for hundreds and hundreds of hours validates them as "cause" for any and all ills the client suffers from. It's the same problem as endless engram running brought about in the 1950s. Whether one validates the engram bank or the spirit world as the cause of all ills, the result is that the apparent cause becomes stronger and stronger and tends to overwhelm the client as he is continuously put at effect. "Cause over life", as we understand it, should mean the client is in charge, not the spirit world.

GPMs and Beingness

What is not being addressed on the current OT levels (advanced levels) is Goals Problems Masses. The Goals Problems Masses came about as a result of playing aberrative games, getting into conflicts, and somehow occasionally forming and holding onto dichotomies of identities involved, own IDs and the opposing ones. This phenomenon has gone on before the beginning of time and before this universe.

In auditing GPMs, one addresses the stuck identities which have formed mental ridges, circuits, and valences in the mind. No doubt, there are a large number of entities attached to these IDs of the client's own creation. In auditing GPMs, we find there is little or no liability attached to ignoring these entities until they occasionally need to be addressed in repair actions. Usually, one will experience a shifting and blowing off of masses after a session. In our experience, when concentrating on the GPMs, one takes care of the structure the entities hold onto. The entity case we see as the "me-too case". The entities react to what's already there. They copy things or react to them in various ways. The entities are usually utterly at effect. We understand them mainly as a recording medium for the client's experiences and postulates. They either resonate with the client's own case or don't resonate as the case may be. In auditing the GPMs, we address the client's own postulates which form the backbone and structure of his case. Once this structure is taken care of and dissolved, the entities blow wholesale without the auditor having to pay much attention to them.

The basic unit of a GPM is an unresolved conflict.
The reader will probably be able to relate to conflicts between a man and a woman. The battle of the sexes seems to have gone on forever and has an archetypical dimension. In modern GPM auditing, one should resolve these old archetypical conflicts, one type of conflict at the time, before looking for other material in "the marriage GPM". A conflict is resolved in the mind by discharging the two identities against each other.

There is another reason we find that extensive Solo NOTs auditing is a liability. It seems that the entities copy the client's own past identities as they can be found in GPMs. To try to "blow them off" doesn't make any sense at all. This action tends to fragment the client. The right approach, in our book, is to inspect the postulates that hold the pairs of opposed IDs and all the other parts of the GPMs in place. These structures dissolve rather easily with the right approach. Most of what happens is that attention units belonging to the client are recovered and integrated as part of himself. Along with that, the entities copying the IDs, may or may not blow. This takes care of itself once the client's own postulates and aberrations are handled. However, when one tries to "blow" IDs consisting mainly of own-trapped attention units, we get a fragmentation or a "buttered-all-over-the-universe" experience and case condition, to use one of Ron Hubbard's expressions.

NOTs at its best

NOTs was, and is, a marvelous tech that has performed miracles over the years. In hindsight, it is a limited technique of finding and clearing up the "me-too case". The tech had its most spectacular results when it first came out. At the time, and prior to NOTs, auditing engrams with Dianetics on OTs was the rule. It had resulted in much misowned charge on many OT cases. The client had been trying to run and erase charge that belonged to the entities. NOTs clears this charge up in short order and takes a load off the case. It also addresses many other causes of misowned charge. Once the misowned charge is handled, however, one should recognize that this tech has done its job, and its future role is repairs and occasional clean-ups. What happened when it was overextended into endless Solo NOTs, was that charge that was the client's own creation now got misassigned as being the charge of entities. It's not a new idea in healing nor in auditing that too much of a good thing can cause harm. NOTs was actually designed to take care of Dianetics' overruns in the first place. One unproven datum that led into this mess in the first place, was the assertion that once the person was Clear there was absolutely nothing left of the person's own bank. The timetrack, the track of the clients experiences through the ages, according to Ron Hubbard was completely gone.

The current definition of Clear is, "a Being who no longer has his own reactive mind", the implication being that what is left of reactivity and aberration belongs to the entities. This seems, in hindsight, to be wishful thinking. Incident running of the client's own timetrack, including engram running, seems quite possible after Clear with techniques other than New Era Dianetics, such as Robert Ducharme's R3X. Part of the problem could have been that New Era Dianetics went earlier similar too fast. As the bank after Clear is rather light and fluid, compared to solid on non-clears, the client and the session could easily fly off the tracks, so to speak, and land the client in the entity case, the always present "me-too" crowd. We think that's what happened.

The conclusion we have come to, running various versions of GPM tech, is that there is still an almost endless amount of track and data in the bank. It's all there and waiting to be run. One can concentrate on running the IDs that are stacked up in the GPMs or one can choose to run a lot of track. In one GPM process we used, we audited endless track incidents as "prior confusions" to the GPM goals. It brought up all kinds of whole-track adventures similar to what the readers may recall from their own Dianetics auditing.

GPMs and NOTs

In NOTs one handles entities, one at the time, with valence technique. One basically isolates one body thetan at a time and flips it out of the valence it is stuck in (a stuck viewpoint, so to speak). The process gets the body thetan back in its own valence, its free-spirited beingness. There are many obvious questions the NOTs materials avoid. Where do the Body Thetans come from? Why are they stuck to the client? Where are they going? What kinds of beings are they? How many kinds of entities are there? These are some existential questions that have been around still unanswered.

We will not say that our studies have revealed the final answers to all of that. We have, however, found some workable truths that directly can be applied to processing. Bear with us if you disagree. We have to say it as we see it and ask you to check it out on your own.

Function and structure

As we see it, the resistive part of the NOTs case is the GPM case seen through a microscope. You see the tiny and isolated parts rather than the full picture. The NOTs techniques and data fall short as far as the super-structures of the GPMs are concerned. An early maxim of Hubbards was "Function monitors structure". This is the same law as "Postulates are senior to the physical universe"; "Purpose is senior to form"; "Considerations are senior to mechanics". What this means is that any creation or organism has come about due to one or many postulates. The creation or organism will take on the outward form that the postulates somehow dictated. To unlock unwanted creations, one should therefore find the rationale and postulates that created them and, most likely, still are active and keeping them created. Finding the postulates at work would include finding their right origin. To unlock the resistive part of the NOTs case, one has to understand client valences and the basic structure of GPMs. The following two definitions of GPMs in the Technical Dictionary are to the point: 4. Goals Problem Mass: the problem created by two or more opposing ideas which being opposed, balanced, and unresolved, make a mass. It's a mental energy mass. (SH Spec 83, 6612C06) 5. items (valences) in opposition to one another. Any pair of these items, in opposition to each other, constitute a specific problem. (HCOB 23 Nov 62).

So we have two opposing postulates. These postulates are the goals or obsessions held by the valences or identities as we prefer to call them. These identities/valences are not BTs. They are typically past IDs the client has occupied or opposed. Tech dictionary definition (3) states: 3. a GPM: constitutes of items, beingnesses, that the person has been and has fought. (SH Spec 137, 6204C24) The BTs, as we see it, are not these valences. They are building materials that, in part, make up these identities. BTs are usually rather inert and benign. They are at total effect and do very little by themselves. They can be held in place by the client; they can be energized by the client and perform their brand of obsession or compulsion. Also, they seem to be able to hold data; we see them as a recording medium of sorts the Being often uses inadvertently. As far as the client's case is concerned, an entity can be found in one of three conditions: (1) It can be inert, i.e., it does not affect the case but is present; (2) It can be restimulated. This restimulation occurs only along the lines of what it's already stuck in. There is a simple on/off choice of conditions: it's either keyed in or it's keyed out; (3) It can be absent or "blown". By being restimulated or keyed in, an entity holds data. By removing whatever restimulated it in the first place, it is keyed out; the entity becomes inert or blows; it returns to its origin or whatever. What happens to them should be of secondary concern to the practitioner, if her objective is to make the client well. Being on some spiritual mission of freeing entities, is not part of what auditing should be about. In GPM auditing, the entities should be recognized and granted beingness for what they are but need only be addressed occasionally as part of repair actions. What we are saying, is that the entity population on a case is mainly a medium that responds to the client's postulates and considerations. The large majority (an estimation would be over 90%) are fragments of other Beings that are alive and well elsewhere. Release the entities and we don't see an explosion in the population of humans. The only social impact releasing entities has, as far as we are concerned, is to have less dispersed and fragmented thetans all around, including the client. As fragments of theta, body thetans are best understood as stray attention units that got caught up in other thetans' cases for whatever reason. It could be old mutual involvement, similarity of games or misidentifications (A=A=A). Theta, according to Scientology axiom 1 is not located originally. It has no location, mass or wavelength. What locates spiritual energy (theta) is interest and fixated attention. Interest and attention require that one chooses a point of view, thus they become located.

What we have learned

What the author has learned from all this studying and research could be summed up this way:

1. The client's valences are senior to any entity found on his case.
2. Entities can be found as elements in a given valence. The entities flavor the valence with color, eccentricity, and oddities, but the postulates that determine if the entities are triggered, keyed in, keyed out or simply gone are the client's own.

We see the entities as elements in a larger structure or group, like the members in this school band. Each member colors the band but the overall beingness of the band is determined by outside forces, such as the school's music director.

In the mind we have senior structures in the form of valences or IDs, that again are part of a larger GPM structure. One has to address the senior structures and the postulates behind them to resolve matters.

3. These postulates are the types found in GPMs. The reason they stick, and thus prevent the entities from blowing, can be resolved within the GPM theory. One valence in a dichotomy is hung up

against another. They are hung up in a way so they form an age old unresolved conflict. Once this dichotomy is resolved, the client can let go of the valences, and the elements they are built of are no longer needed and will thus easily come off as well.

4. That a person has gone clear is no guarantee that the GPM case is gone. The way to overcome the GPM case is to address it and handle all there is to handle. It does not just "blow" as the result of other auditing, be it Grades, Dianetics, addressing implants or entities. Any auditing takes charge off the case in general. To dissolve or deconstruct things that persist, the exact postulate holding it in place, needs to be found.

5. The GPM case is a very basic level of case. It's a record of the games of life as they took place since before the beginning of time. What can be found in the mind as GPMs, is the residue in the form of mental masses of what the client has been and done and fought against on the whole track. This residue can manifest itself as ridges, circuits, and valences just as described in the Briefing Course materials by Hubbard. A GPM is a layered record of old unresolved conflicts. The layers of these masses are held together by a common underlying passion or theme as explained in earlier articles. The themes are passions the being just wouldn't give up on even after crashing into a brick wall of opposition. Rather than giving up on the theme, the being kept finding new ways and tactics to pursue it. Each tactic was a goal inside the GPM. As each of these tactics were met by opposition, we got layer after layer of dichotomies. The masses brought about by these conflicts remain created and are basically energized by the passion for the theme. We find the client's ID smack up against the opposition, over and over, in the pattern we call a line-plot. These masses should be addressed, one conflict at a time, and be resolved.

6. It's risky business to try to strictly follow the line-plots. At any given time a multitude of themes are in play in the hodgepodge called Life. The best approach is to unburden the GPM case, one dichotomy at a time. Each available dichotomy can be successfully processed to its own end phenomena, and should be, before looking for the next readily available pair. Once several dichotomies within the same theme have successfully been processed, the whole GPM may collapse, as it was a delicate balance in the first place.

In conclusion

Having originally done over 1200 hours of NOTs and Solo NOTs combined, and of late about 300 hours of GPM auditing, the author thinks he is entitled to express an informed opinion. We found that the NOTs case is a surface charge phenomenon. We like to call it the "me-too case". Granted, there is quite a lot of "surface", but the main reason the "me-too case" stuck in the first place, is that it helped model and form the IDs of the GPM case. It added color, eccentricity, and emphasis, intended or unintended, to these IDs. The NOTs auditing is an unburdening action. It unburdens the client's GPM structures and valences. Removing entities is comparable to removing locks from the engram case. As we know from engram running, one shouldn't unburden forever but start in on the real stuff and erase it. When we talk NOTs and GPMs, the real stuff is the self-created structures and valences of the GPMs. The basic unit is the dichotomy of two opposing IDs. Once the GPMs are available, one should go to work and remove them. Once they are removed, the real reason for most of the NOTs case is gone. The most detailed record of the anatomy of GPMs is found in Hubbard materials on the subject. Since there were so many different trial-and-error attempts, it is not that easy to unscramble. The basic flaw in processing them in the 1960s was that Hubbard wanted to do too much too fast. The right approach, we find, is to fully handle one dichotomy at a time. In following the lineplots right away, red-hot dichotomies were often left behind, and this led to errors in finding opposite IDs.

As explained in "Adventurous Routine 2-12", another reason was that endless listing was erroneously considered the way to discharge identities. Yet, when a gibbering hot dichotomy was finally found, it was not flattened but was left rock-slamming. In almost all the early techniques, much more charge was restimulated than blown. It resulted in bogged auditing, blown students, and severe illness as the grim results in many instances. If one considers one dichotomy the basic objective of auditing, success becomes possible. One has to flatten and resolve one dichotomy at a time and treat it as the basic process. The GPMs as well as the entities are there. They interact in ways that haven't been well understood. There is, of course, much more to learn about this. What I want to press home is that the Pre OT case (the case after Clear) is not 'entities from here on out'. Our cases as they exist in present time aren't simply the result of grim conspiracies either. The next level known, as far as I can tell, was isolated and researched by Hubbard in the 1960s. It just wasn't tackled with the right technology at the time. Applying what we learned from later Hubbard research helped a lot. Putting it all together was done by various researchers in the Freezone. The GPMs are real. They need to be handled if one wants to go free for real. It may be a lot of extra work. We have found it an adventure so far. Some of us are in for the long haul and for what it takes. To those of you that are of that mind-set, we have dedicated this article series and website.

Chapter 12: GPM Series 6

The Karma Buster Process

Explore the Dark Side of Your Karma

What we address in this processing is ***"identities the person has been or has fought."***
The quote is one of Ron Hubbard's definitions for GPMs. These identities, thus, would include own identities and any identity the person has had some kind of problematic relationship with, present and past.

Character: In Karma Buster we address Characters. Synonyms in Scientology are 'valences', 'ridges', 'terminals', 'opposition terminals,' identities,' 'circuits,' machinery.'

Elsewhere we mainly used the term 'identities' or IDs. Sometimes these ridges have lost all of their 'personality' and lifelike characteristics because they have been utterly squashed so we only have left what can be identified as a ridge or a mental mass. A Character, in this context, is understood to be a fictitious personality. That is how it is used in literature and story telling. What routinely happens during Karma Buster is that what is first contacted as a mass or ridge can be developed into an identity or character. Once its 'personality' is established and recovered, the entity is addressed as a character, a beingness.

Definition in Miriam Webster: Character:

7 a : a person marked by notable or conspicuous traits <quite a character> **b :** one of the persons of a drama or novel **c :** the personality or part which an actor recreates <an actress who can create a character convincingly> **d :** characterization especially in drama or fiction **e :** person, individual <a suspicious character>

The characters we are interested in are *not* defined as BTs or Clusters. The characters we are interested in are seen as creations of the client*. The client is ultimately cause and his postulates, efforts and emotions are the senior factors of anything accumulated in his theta-body or space. The entities we are interested in are holograms or simulations of persons the client has been or fought; but they are often squashed and denied into small mental ridges.

One theory of why the client carries them along is that the client uses or has used them to do certain routine tasks or uses them as stimulus-response mechanisms to handle dangerous situations. They are "bureaucrats of the mind" with one single function: the execution of one certain function or goal. Like a bureaucrat they are stuck with or stuck in a 'Hat.' It has a goal and a detailed description of all the administrative functions, including its 'valuable final products.' So rather than operating on the goal only, they operate on a whole array of functions or hat. When the client moved on, he forgot to "dis-create" them (to as-is them.) Later on, these 'old hats' can become very inapplicable and aberrating**. In the true GPM structures you will see the client forming new hats and vigorously fighting his old hats that now are identified with the enemy.

* The Characters or Entities we address are consistent with the description given by Ron Hubbard in "A History of Man." Here is a quote: They [the entities] are probably just compartments of the mind which, cut off, begin to act as if they were persons. Here is an inexhaustible source of study and speculation which I leave to another."

We believe this study and the processes developed from it will answer the questions that could be raised.

** Another quote from *A History of Man*: "The Theta Being is the "I", it is WHO the client is. If all the entities and beingnesses of the client were hydrogen balloons locked up inside him and each had a name and identity, the auditor might be confused and the client IS confused as to who "I" is. But if the client were suddenly opened and all the balloons let loose, the "I" balloon would be the spiritual being, it would be who the client always thought he was anyway. All others are simply modifiers." And "...unless the client is obviously insane, these sub-personalities are not distinctly units in themselves but only color the activities of the spiritual being."

===

Another way of looking at these characters can be extracted from Logics (logic 4 and 21 quoted below.) The entities are 'facsimiles of states of being.' It means we use these simulated beingnesses as representations, facsimiles or holograms to calculate the behavior of others. Apparently this function of creating simulations of perceived dangerous characters and enemies is an everyday natural function of the mind. We use it to create simulations of co-workers, celebrities and loved ones as well. It is used in predicting behaviors and having ready-made responses. They are all representations used in all the calculations of behaviors and efforts needed to predict life with its dangers and pleasures. It is a form of "behavioral mathematics", if you will. We use it in order to predict life, survive and, hopefully, thrive.

(Logic 4: A datum is a facsimile of states of being, states of not being, actions or inactions, conclusions, or suppositions in the physical or any other universe. |Comments: 'Facsimile' is the central word. According to the dictionary it means, exact copy, such as a photo or photo copy. From Latin 'fac' and 'similar', originally meaning 'make similar'. The human mind is capable of making facsimiles of anything and does so in order work with problems on a mental level.

Logic 21. Mathematics are methods of postulating or resolving real or abstract data in any universe and integrating by symbolization of data, postulates and resolutions.
In Logic 4 we saw how the human mind works with facsimiles to solve problems. Mathematics takes this principle to the extreme by using symbols and formulas. Mathematics defines the abstract 'universe' to which it applies. It then defines things so they can be expressed numerically. Now you can do very precise calculations and predictions in that limited 'universe'. It's like a computer program. It lacks human emotion and intelligence but is very useful in its special field.)

These 'facsimiles of states of being' are not "the GPM structure" as such, but it is most certainly the pool from where GPM terminals (characters) are recruited, so to speak, when the right "chemistry of adhesive forces" is present. When self-created identities get stuck or hung up against each other in a fight we certainly have a serious problem; we get a pair of GPM terminals. Over eons of time we have gotten stuck with a very little percentage of these types of problems.

The pairs/problems form reactive structures with each other. These structures are called the line-plots. The adhesive force is goals in opposition or conflict. The opposing goals as an adhesive force operate outside of time. Another adhesive force, we believe, is the clients hunger for a story or a destiny. You can extract all the dramas of the world from the GPM case. Your own GPM case comprises the blueprint for your destiny, your Karma. The timeless nature of the GPM goals means that they can get activated at any time the client operates on similar goals and purposes. The goals in a GPM form a pattern of related conflicts. It is a chain of problems and solutions. We have layer after layer of opposing goals. The layers stick together as well, as a goal in one layer has a stuck conflict with a goal in the next layer. All goals and conflicts in one GPM are related to the same topic or theme. It's "all about sex", "all about military life", "all about politics", or whatever. Once one layer has become an irresolvable problem of equal forces, a new solution is found (a new but related course or goal) which starts the forming of the next layer. What we get is a goals-problems-mass, or simply a "super problem." The opposing and adhesive forces cause the 'facsimiles of being' to be squashed completely as do the clients efforts to discard of them by denying them. We now have a client with mental ridges.

When he tries to operate as an OT (free spirit) he soon collides with all these skeletons in the closet. They comprise his "Karma."

Getting Started

The way to get started on taking this mess apart is to address this lifetime conflicts the client is stuck in. That is what is explained on the DEEP Page. It is also what the Hubbard process R2-12 sought to address.

The main tool used in Karma Buster is Effort Processing (developed by Ron Hubbard in 1951.) We use Effort Processing on the two opposing entities, one after the other. There isn't much written on how Effort Processing was originally run. The best reference thus far found, is in the book "A History of Man" (1951). It describes in chapter 2 how "entities" can and should be run on Effort processing. Another issue is "Self-Determined Effort Processing" from 1951. It goes more to how to run it -- as does the book, Advanced Procedures and Axioms (1952). Although the principles are laid out we have found new ways to use these principles. To get it to an effective tech, different approaches have been applied to see what works the best.

From glossary: A Character is like a hired bureaucrat. It has one duty and basic function only: to succeed in executing the goal it has been entrusted with by the Being. A whole hat or organization has been formed around this goal. It is therefore not enough just to address the goal. Also, like you see in government, the "bureaucrat of the mind" will hang around and draw a paycheck in the form of spiritual (theta) energy forever if nobody higher up releases it from its duties. It is a machine or robot the Being has built and granted life to -- originally out of convenience or perceived necessity (the latter can happen after traumatic incidents and shocks.) But now it has taken on a life of its own and may later on be in severe conflict with its master or with other entities.

Chapter 13: GPM Series 7
DEEP Character Clearing and the GPM Case

Introduction

We as spiritual Beings have played an almost infinity of different games and roles in this universe. The reason to join in games in the first place was basically to experience engagement and excitement. To play a role in a game seemed better than just "sitting on a cloud" in a serene and ideal state and listen to harp music and the whisper of eternity. The motto we follow now seems to be "There must be a game!" and "Any game is better than no game!" We experience engagement, fun and the full range of emotions from playing games. Unfortunately, "All games are aberrative." Since a certain type of game (say, "to teach", "to have a family", "to fight for justice") tends to deteriorate over the eons, Beings become more and more aberrated by keeping on playing them. Yet, they hold onto all the experiences they gather but in a reactive way. They keep it so they know what to do next time that game comes around. But they also accumulate reactive experiences and behavioral patterns that may take control in very irrational ways. In this manner the Being accumulates what is known as the GPM case.

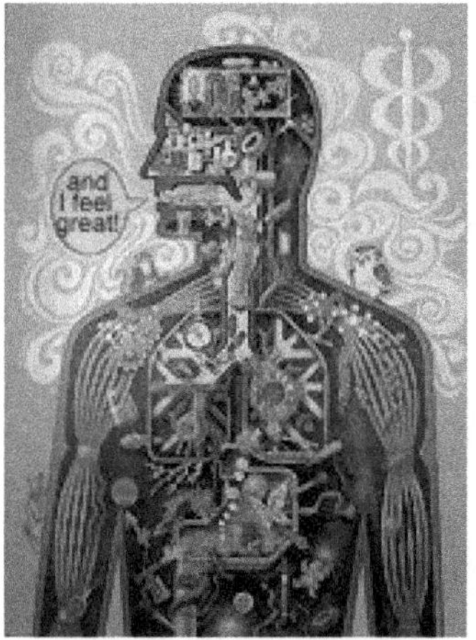

The GPM case exists as potential ridges and energies in and around the body. It may be energized and ridged up when triggered.

Stuck Identities

The GPM Case is basically conflicting identities the Being is stuck in and the efforts, emotions and impulses of these identities. The mental masses and energies that is the record of these conflicts make up complex unresolved problems of very long duration on the case. The Being, from ideally being a free spirit capable of being anything at will, has become a fragmented and complex Being, a congregation of stuck viewpoints out of alignment and somewhat short-circuited. The efforts exerted by these conflicting and colliding identities (or stuck roles in games of the past) build up mental masses and tensions that can result in all kinds of unwanted sensations, pains, etc. This can result in physical illness in some cases. The ideas and patterns engraved in these masses can result in aberrated ideas and behavior, even insanity.

We define "Identity" this way: It is a way to organize skills and experience, so they are instantly available to the Being when needed. Before the identity was formed there was a goal expressing the "want to succeed" (or sometimes "want to have" or end product) in a certain area. A doctor would have a goal like "to heal people", (by end product: to make healthy people); an architect a goal like "to build houses". (By end product: to make nicely built houses). So there is a basic goal and an identity that go together and they define the game and the role to play. An identity is obviously also a substitute for the Being. From a free Being's viewpoint, an identity is a piece in a game (as for instance a piece in a chess game) he controls and identifies with.

Hats and Characters

A fully analytical identity is called a Hat. Wearing one's hat means one knows one's business and is competent in that area. The Being is a competent player in that particular game. "The wearing of one's hat" is wearing all the skills needed to perform a certain job or function competently. There is no need to consult books, etc. When one knows the hat fully, one can "instinctively" and instantly execute the job competently. One is a competent player in that game.

A more reactive identity is called a Character. It contains impulses, emotions and ideas on how to handle a certain type of situation or opponent. It is mainly that kind of identities we are interested in in DEEP Character Clearing. Characters are viewpoints split off from the main Being at some point. They are substitutes for the Being. They contain much reactivity in the form of efforts, impulses, emotions, feelings and strange ideas.

DEEP Character Clearing clears up the reactivity and all the irrational automatic impulses one acts on in handling situations, other people and life. Once again these cut off viewpoints become integrated into the Being as free life-force under the Being's control.

A basic unit of the GPM is the goal and the identity that excecutes it. In DEEP Character Clearing we use the terms "Main Effort" for goal and "Character" for the ID. Identities with the goal "to catch fish" can be very different based on culture, technology and experiences; the word Character reflects that. In DEEP we are mainly interested in the characters as they contain all the mass while the goals derive from a non-physical decision or postulate. Still, getting the goal /main effort of a Character is of vital importance. The goal is actually the life force that accumulates the mass.

Fragmentation and Integrity

When the person first comes in for processing the case state he or she is in could best be characterized with this word: Fragmented. We are not talking about "multiple personality" except in very rare cases. We are talking about ordinary people and we find that their life-force is locked up in the identities the person has been in past games, lives and scenarios. The free life force is also locked up in identities the person has fought. These identities have since been reduced to small packages and the Being has put a lid on it all. From being a life size drama it has been reduced to an ambivalent attitude towards certain subjects or persons; to an occasional headache and odd and inexplicable impulses. Through DEEP Character Clearing, the locked up life-force becomes once again freed up and at the Being's disposal in present time. The person can as a result be exactly what is needed in a certain situation using "fresh" life-force and without being caught up in all the odd and old identities and characters who offer complicated solutions in various life situations – solutions and circuits that most frequently are completely out of date and inapplicable.

GPMs a Bureaucracy of the Mind

The GPM case is basically built on goals. A goal is a long term strategy or solution to a life situation. It is a statement of something desirable or wanted one is striving to obtain. All goals are thus decisions of creating a future and thus time. These GPM goals, as they now exist, contain a lot of effort. They express themselves in somewhat obsessive and automatic actions and behaviors. We are often dealing with a system of pulling and pushing in opposing or conflicting directions. It has become a system of "bureaucratic solutions" to life situations that existed. By bureaucratic solution is meant: Each element (consisting of a goal and its identity) was established as a routine practice at some point. It was left in place even after the life situation shifted completely. Now it keeps nagging the person as irrational actions and impulses that don't apply to his/her current situation. As you see in groups that have decayed and fragmented, the different members of the group fight each other, each holding a stuck viewpoint and incapable of seeing the viewpoints of the other members. Sometimes these conflicts are overruled and swept aside by a "strong man" or dictator, but the underlying conflicts still exist in suppressed form and steal maybe 90% of the power or life-force available.

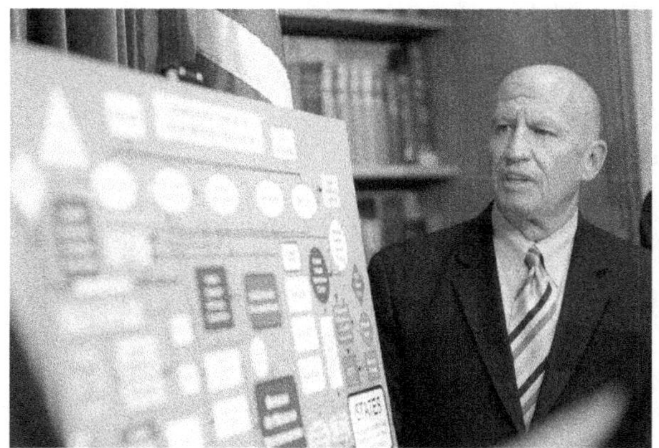

A bureaucracy operates on a fixated set of goals. It does not on its own adapt to new situations. The typical bureaucrat takes no-nonsense from anyone as he knows he does what he is supposed to. This is very comparable to the characters and their main efforts we find in the GPMs. Each character operates in a mechanical mode. The bureaucracy as such, without any outside help, becomes a non viable system of circuits and machinery.

Each of these once long term goals started out as a bright strategy or solution to a life situation. A better future was postulated. Over time the goal deteriorated to less and less ambitious expectations and eventually got abandoned – or they became irrelevant as life situations changed.

The life energy that got fed into them was reduced, yet it works as a secret leak or nullifying of power or life-force. (In a malfunctioning bureaucracy you often get a clear illustration of how this infighting results in nullification of power.)

The goal decayed and became a totally automatic routine; it sort of petrified. From being an alive decision and strategy for a better future it became a heavy effort out of control.

A main goal (as found in a profession, career, lifestyle, personal or social ambition) was the basic force and power behind the forming and building of the identity. As mentioned, an identity is a handy way to organize relevant skills and experiences in order to survive and thrive along a certain goal line. As time went on, incidents and experiences added mass to it. It accumulated negative and traumatic experiences, adding more mass and aberration. Over the long career of the Being in this universe, many identities were formed this way, typically one at the time. That was what the Being was living. He spent a life as a baker and formed an identity as a baker with all the skills, experience and knowledge that takes; then another one, etc.

GPMs and Roles

A Being can be anything and it seems most Beings have tried just about anything. A Being could have been a police man for many lives, then a robber for several lifetimes, then a career as a judge over several lives, then a jail keeper or hang man career, then a role as victim of crime, then returning to being a police man once more, etc., etc. These identities or roles all exist in rudimentary form around the Being as fragments in conflict or fragments nullifying each other in what is perceived as mental ridges. These identities could also be considered a resource and data-base for handling just about any situation and that is probably why the Being holds onto all this.

As all these identities and experiences added up and never really got sorted out, the Being got absorbed in complexities. One identity (such as robber) got hung up against other identities (such as police man, judge or victim) and formed what is called a GPM – or as we prefer to call it – a goals identity super-problem (GISP).

A Being has tried just about anything in terms of identities. Therefore when playing a game, such as being a robber, the opposing side will often get triggered, such as being a jail keeper. With a few associated but conflicting goals and their identities in play, we soon have a Goals-Identities Super Problem (or GISP), the DEEP term for GPMs.

The Running of DEEP Character Clearing

The way DEEP Character Clearing works is to isolate one character (ID) and its main effort (goal) and run it; then find the main character or effort in conflict with the original one and in turn run that one out. The processor asks for certain types of polarities involved in such a character as well as emotions, supporting efforts, decisions and thoughts that all are part of the identity package. Sometimes the one side can be handled completely and the other side seems to have faded away in the process and lost its influence on the case. The End Point of any such action is that the split off fragment or identity once again has become free life-force at the Being's disposal. The Being can now at will be that character and hat when life situations call for it. When one keeps up handling all available identities and polarities a whole layer of conflicting efforts and conflicting characters can be run out on the case and by then one has gotten rid of the accessible part of the GPM case (the GISP case).

What the Being will experience after such processing is a much greater ability to grant beingness to others. The life force locked up in these old games, these old goals and identities has, once again, been reunited with the Being who created them. This means more life force available and a tremendous move up the tone scale. The Being will see in himself a much greater ability to adapt his own beingness to difficult or new situations. Instead of his mind and spirit being a split up conglomerate or a fragmentation into a big malfunctioning bureaucracy of old solutions, the mind and spirit will consist of free life-force and constructive imagination, images and thinking made in present time and resulting in new abilities. The Being can routinely experience this: at will to be anything the situation requires and with great compassion be able to permeate opponents and enemies and get the opponent to brighten up and self-determinedly change his stubborn and uncooperative ways.

There are a number of ways to get started in finding one side of a goals-identity super problem (GISP). Once that is found and run, the other side will usually be easily available. One can then find other layers (polarities) related to the same goals and identities or find something else that now is available. We have found with this technique the risks are very minimal. You run what you find and flatten it and something else will offer itself to be run.

Some of these goals and identities will be central pieces of the case, others may be marginal and only in play as synthetic identities. That is fine. That is also how it works in life. Not all polarities found are basic conflicts of archetypical dimensions. That is fine too. It all serves to unburden the basic goals and conflicts that have had defining importance to the Being's career in this and earlier universes.

> ***"What the Being will experience after such processing is a much greater ability to grant beingness to others. The life force locked up in these old games, these old goals and identities have, once again, been reunited with the Being who created them."***

What is run out directly in DEEP Character Clearing are the characters (IDs) that are built around one particular goal or strategy and its contributing efforts. There is a main effort (the goal) and a long series of contributing efforts (the organization behind effectively executing the main goal or effort.)

All these efforts are considered "character traits" as they add up to what we call a character. They add up to the hat that is being worn in order to succeed at a particular goal. The contributing efforts we are looking for make up an organization board of sorts.

In order to catch fish (main effort, goal) and be a good fisherman (character, ID) there are many functions that need to work. The fisherman is dealing with all kinds of forces, tools and practical problems; cultural factors and prevailing fixed ideas. He must have a set of responses in place in order to be successful as a fisherman. Since these hats routinely are way out of present time and place there is a lot of aberration contained in them.

The problems involved can also be compared to an old sleepy (or angry and infighting) bureaucracy where the one officer is unaware of the others. The bureaucracy has fragmented. Each single bureaucrat knows that he is right and he knows that he must carry out his duties regardless of any opposition. It is this fragmentation that nullifies old bureaucracies' power and it is a similar simmering of old forgotten conflicts that nullifies a Being's power.

There are different entrances into DEEP Character Clearing. Each way of entering can be organized into a rundown (set of actions; protocol). At this time, one uses the approach that is most appropriate to what the person offers as the main issue. The most obvious starting point is to take a list of individuals that are perceived as troublesome or hostile to the person. These are in some way in opposition to the person (or perceived to be) and thus make good processing material as counter-poles. When doing that, the "other side" of the polarity is often perceived as self in a special capacity or situation.

In addressing this, we address two main stumbling blocks to case progress:

1) We handle any ongoing conflicts with the upsets, problems and guarded secrets involved (out rudiments.)
2) We handle any ongoing suppression on the case, also known as PTSness, at its root cause.

The main difference between running this action and other actions of DEEP Character Clearing is in how you go about getting into the technique. Therefore there will be some unique steps, mainly at the beginning of an action.

What is taken up as the first action is individuals in the person's present time the person has difficulties with, meaning lots of problems, conflicts, upsets, personality clashes, etc.

This can be expanded to troublesome individuals the person has encountered earlier in life.

Also, scanning the person's history for old conflicts and major upsets will reveal much material.

Chapter 14: GPM Series 8
DEEP Character Clearing —Basic Procedure

with explanations. Revised April 2020

Content

Introduction

in DEEP Character Clearing (DCC) we are dealing in archetypes, meaning eternal roles we take on ourselves or are battling. Typically, what we take up first is important characters that are troublesome to the introspector (client), such as a difficult parent, a boss, an ex-spouse, etc. But beyond that, we are dealing in characters or identities 'the person has fought and the person has been' throughout his or her existence of millions of years. Once a troublesome person is handled, we look at the role and identity the person him- or herself took on in the conflict. This is the other side of the game, the polarity. It takes two to dance tango and it takes at least two players to have a conflict or game. By running both sides, the introspector gains a deep insight in the games of life and ultimately in the eternal and repeated games we play.

In principle any character with charge can be run with benefit. It is not always possible to run identities (IDs) as pairs. Some identities were formed in response to a general survival situation and the 'opponent' may be stated as nature, the environment, living conditions, a political situation, etc. For instance, a sailor would typically have the sea as his 'main opponent.' Yet, being or having been a sailor can be a distinct and charged character. If we have a clear own role and identity, say, a farmer, a hunter, an executive, etc. we can run. We have to make sure to get the reactions and viewpoints of others around him/her as we go along. If we run an identity the introspector has fought, and make sure to get the person's own views and reactions to it as we go forward, we can in a similar fashion leave an unfriendly or opponent identity at that. However, the most charged characters exist in pairs. They have become two poles in a battery that produces charge. A better idea is therefore to find the other side of this duality, if at all possible, once the obvious side is handled. When both sides are dissolved the poles in the battery are gone and the charge they generated stops. Another reason to look carefully for the counter-pole is that, if we keep running characters that have fought the introspector, without looking at what the guy did in return, we will soon have a gallery of "bad guys" where the person is the "innocent victim" and this would be very unfortunate. What we have is a very distorted picture of life and the games of life. Therefore, if it is at all possible the identities should be run in pairs – pole and counter-pole.

One usually starts with what is seen as an opponent, a counter-pole. But there are different ways to get into DCC, depending on the issue the person presents. How to deal with different types of issues using DCC is covered in a later chapter. The present write-up is mainly giving the practical data the clearer needs (Clearer is our word for practitioner). The write-up contains also the main procedure with explanations.

The main difference between running the Troublesome Person technique, where we simply take a list of people who have caused our client troubles throughout life, and other actions of DCC, is in how we go about getting into the action. For each technique there will be a unique step at the very beginning of the action designed to find the identities central to the issue.

We assume in the present write-up that what is taken up as the first action is an opponent-identity the introspector has current difficulties with; meaning a relationship with lots of problems, conflicts, upsets, personality clashes, etc. Once that is run we find the introspector's own identity and role in the conflict and run that.

Once present life situations are out of the way the action can be expanded to troublesome characters the person has encountered in earlier life. Also, scanning the person's history and earlier lives of millions of years for old conflicts and major upsets will reveal much material.

As mentioned, we run the introspector's own reactions to the opponent as we go along. That is the first method of discharging the polarity. When that is done it is time to focus fully on the introspector's own reactive role and identity in the conflict. We therefore run the conflict from the introspector's own viewpoint. We see it all through the introspector's own eyes so to speak.

It is worth pointing out, when we are running other characters than self, we are not addressing the person behind the identity or character. If the item is "mother" it means, that it is not the person's mother who is receiving clearing, nor is it mother who answers the questions. She may be long gone for that matter. It is the character 'mother' in the introspector's own mind that is addressed and that provides the answers. Interestingly enough, 'Character' means originally 'Imprint' as on the surface of a coin. This is well suited for our purposes as it is the imprint that 'mother' has left on the person's mind that we address. This may be a much distorted picture of the real person, the mother. However, what we do in DCC is to clear and integrate this 'character' into the person's sphere of control, influence and responsibility. All the prejudice, distortions and non-confront disappear. And instead of dealing with this distorted character 'mother' the person is dealing with the real person 'mother' next time they meet.

The Goal of DCC

Another common meaning of 'Character' is: Integrity; 'qualities of honesty, courage, sincerity and the like.' As we progress in running DCC the introspector will gain in this regard. The reason is simple. The temporary or 'false' characters get handled; their fixed ways of thinking, feeling, acting and reacting get dissolved. Due to this the person becomes more and more flexible in thought and emotion and closer to his/her ideal good self of high integrity, etc.

Theoretically the ultimate goal of DCC would be that the Being would be above identity entirely; simply capable of assuming any identity at will when needed. The Being as such is above identity and character, pure cause and potential if you will. This is what is called Nirvana in Buddhism.

In practice we run DCC until there are no more charged counter-poles and dramatized roles in sight. This by itself is a very desirable state where the Being is at a high cause level and willing to deal with all kinds of people and situations—without prejudice or back-off. Indeed, the person can meet the world with a flexible and open mind and spirit and join and engage in new games that are meaningful and fun.

The Sections

The procedure is divided into a series of sections or major steps. It has not been possible to lay it all out in rigid rote actions that simply can be followed in number order.

The clearer needs to have an understanding of what each section accomplishes. The clearer then uses some or all of the techniques listed in that section to accomplish that result. Sometimes the clearer may need other techniques from the tool box as well. If there isn't a good understanding on the part of the clearer of what he/she is dealing with and how to address it intelligently, the action will accomplish far less than what it is capable of. It is therefore important that the clearer knows the tools and has a practical understanding of when and how to use them.

At first glance the procedure may seem overly long. Our declared goal is however to provide enough techniques to bring about a full resolution, a dissolvement or deconstruction, of the characters encountered. That is brought about when any obsession and automaticity is fully replaced by self-determined control over the character. We have not settled for simply bringing temporarily relief. As the clearer works with DCC, he/she will soon learn how things can be speeded up if little or no charge is found to be dealt with. One can also find that certain identities blow rather quickly and only part of the procedure is needed.

On the other hand, the clearer may encounter DEEP elements that offer themselves for the running with other tools than those listed. Any distinct emotion, feeling, thought, decision, action or reaction the introspector sits with can, when the immediate technique is flattened, be taken up with for instance Repeat and Tell, Dialogue tool or other tools from the DEEP tool box.

As a practical matter, we recommend that the clearer uses the write-up as a computer file that can be scrolled as he/she progresses. In this manner the clearer simply scrolls down and follows the instructions. There is no need to try remembering the procedure by heart.

Section I. Identifying the Character as an Energy-Mass

<u>Finding the Troublesome Character as an Energy-Mass.</u>

The first step is to isolate the mental masses, subtle energies, etc. in the introspector's mind and space that represent the counter-pole, the troublesome person. (It is called "blue character" in the illustrated introduction to DCC.)

These phenomena we call the Energy-Masses. They are isolated and developed using some or all of the techniques in section I.

Note 1: *the Optional techniques* throughout this write-up should be tried at least once with each introspector. Some techniques work very well for a certain person while others don't. So try them out and find the helpful ones for that particular introspector.

Items that are marked with a star (*) are the principal techniques that are used in nearly all cases.

***I-1. "Get the concept of [character]"**

(The following is to get in contact with the mental representation existing in the introspector's mind, not to get in contact with a real person the introspector may have named.)

***I-2a. Tune into it and hold it.**
***I-2b. In your own mind and space,**
"Include any and all energies...,
***I-2c. all masses...,**
***I-2d. All vibrations and flows...**

I-2e. (Optional) **"Give all mental phenomena connected to this main concept a color."** (That reveals its form and size. The introspector can infuse a color or may perceive it as having a certain color.)
***I-3a. "Make it (the character) more solid."** Do this at least 3 times.
***I-3b. "Hold it (the character) still."** Do this at least 3 times.
***I-3c. "Keep it (the character) from going away."** Do this at least 3 times.
***I-3d. The clearer then asks the introspector,**
*** "In terms of energy-masses, what do we have?" or "Describe the energy-masses now."**

Note: In subsequent sessions on the same character steps I-1, 2, 3 are used to get the introspector focused on that character again. The first step is always to call up the character to work on. One can also use other Section I techniques to accomplish that. 3a-3d is called 3xSolid and can be used as a general DEEP tool to process masses.

I-4. (Optional) Using a Marker (Tag). A known conflict with this character is sometimes the best way to pin down that character. "The fight over money we had last year in the back office" would be an example. The person may have an image of the angry face of the boss, the copy machine in the room (the boss being the opponent in the conflict) and can easily tune into that scenario to pin down the exact characters involved. The Marker is in many cases the best and most precise method to keep the person focused on a character, especially when mental ridges and masses are not very real to the introspector.

I-5. (Optional) Draw the energy-masses as a sketch (using a stick man body). The person sits with pen and paper and is asked to draw a sketch of a head and body and illustrate on the drawing where the energy-masses are located and how they impact and behave in and around the body in the introspector's personal space.

I-6. (Optional) Imitate posture of character. Experiment with head- and body posture to turn the character on until you have nailed it. If you get the exact body language it will routinely turn on quite vividly. Pressures and feelings are amplified.

I-7. (Optional) Use hands and fingers. Also use hands and fingers to nail down the energy-masses; pointing and touching areas or spaces where the energy-masses are situated. This can be extremely helpful in terms of realizing that the energy-masses are of physical nature—although very subtle. They are created and maintained by the Being, usually unknowingly. A major part of DCC is to become aware of one's unknowing creations and gain control over them. Duplication and Control of these subtle energies are the two key factors that all the tools and techniques aim to accomplish.

The introspector will usually find that holding the hands and fingers in strategic places on or near the body will amplify or turn on the energy-masses of the character. The person can keep hands there during the running or move them around to continually explore the energy-masses' physical nature and impact. One can place a hand on the back of the head for starters. This can act as a grounding pole. The clearer can then ask the person to point out and physically touch masses, ridges and sensitive areas turned on.

I-8. (Optional) Physical Description. One can also use additional questions to pinpoint locations in and around the body. One can ask to form (does it have a geometrical form?), texture and structure, vibration, color, weight, sometimes temperature, etc. to nail it down, even taste, smell and sound will do the trick in some cases.

Section II. Getting into Communication

We have isolated and identified the energy-masses of the character in question. It seems to have a subtle life of its own. We are not talking pathology. We are talking about phenomena we find in active and well-functioning people. It seems we model the world and its players this way so we can respond and react quickly on what is coming our way. If we had to figure it all out from scratch each time, we would long since be beaten or be dead. The only problem with the mechanism is that our models need to be updated. Our understanding of what is a model and what is objective reality needs to be revised from time to time. With DCC we do just that. We gain duplication and control over all these model characters of our own making that we use to understand and respond competently to the exterior world. A first step into all this is to get into good communication with the character we are dealing with.

***II-1.** Have person assume the viewpoint of the character. The clearer uses following question:
(For a moment) take the viewpoint of (the character).
(In that role/as such) How would you describe yourself?
(Clearer acknowledges answers)

* Run the DEEP package of the character if available.

*** II-2. Dialogue**

We use the well-known DEEP tool of Hello-OK. First we do a few rounds of Hello-OK between character and person. This establishes a communication line along which the messages can travel. It is run this way:

As (ID), say Hello to (your name).	**As (ID), is there s/t you want to say to (your name)?**
As (your name), receive that communication.	**As (your name) receive that.**
As (your name), say Hello to (ID).	**As (your name), is there s/t you want to say to (ID)?**
As (ID) receive that communication.	**As (ID), receive that, etc.**

We use the forms "As (your name)" and "As (the ID)" in order to put some distance between the items and the spiritual Being. Both the personality (the client by name) and the ID are creations of the Being – but not the actual Being itself. The formulation helps the Being take ownership and control of both sides.

*** II-3. We labeled the character [___] Is that still the valid name for it?**

We have gotten to know this character a bit. Maybe we had a working label for it like 'Uncle Jim.' Now we want to make sure we have a good label or name that pinpoints the character in the introspector's mind and thinking and yet allows for the general, the archetypical aspect of the character. It is often a good idea to add an adjective to the name or noun. Instead of 'Uncle Jim' it can be a good idea to name the type; for example, 'Irritating Relative,' 'Sarcastic Uncle,' and the like. The clearer may suggest adding an adjective, but never suggest names or labels. The introspector has to work it out and be happy with it. Hopefully it is short enough so it can be included in questions and instructions. Otherwise, remind the introspector from time to time by saying the label. Having done that, maybe you can get by, by saying "this character" in the instructions if it is a very long label.

Once you have a confirmed name for the character, say it back to the introspector. "The character is ....."

It is a good idea to write it out on a separate piece of note paper as you will have to refer to it frequently later in DCC.

II-4. An opposition character is often heavily invalidated and made appear worse by the introspector. It is said the first victim of war is the truth. In war, we make our enemies into horrible creatures and demons it is ok to kill.

Likewise in our battles with counter-poles. To be able to rise above an opposition character the first requirement is to be able to see it for what it is and have a certain level of understanding. This is what this step is about.

***II-4a. What about (that character) could you accept?**
4b. What about (that character) could you not accept? Till flat.

*** II-5. Find something (else) interesting or peculiar about (that character)**
Accept and acknowledge that.

The idea is to find some traits that can be confronted and accepted. This should be done about 5 times (5 times repeated and accepted/acknowledged by introspector.) It is not something that needs to be run flat.

Section III. Main Goal

A character is organized and built around a main goal. Like a company or organization it is built around main product and purpose. Anything legitimate that goes on in an organization was originally designed and formed to support that basic purpose. So the whole structure exists and keeps functioning based on that. Maybe there are internal things going on that don't support that purpose – but that is another story and these forces are eroding the basic structure. So in an organization or company the basic purpose, the main goal is 'the reason for existing'. Likewise, any profession or job description has a goal or product and an identity to go with it and the same is the case for a character in DCC.

So when we find the basic goal of the character we have taken a big step. The central goal of a character can however 'hide in plain view'. The character has been through so much! It can be so charged up that it can be hard to find or see the basic goal. Below are a series of questions that should unburden it. The person takes the viewpoint of the character and runs the questions. In this way we can sort it all out or unburden the basic goal. The list may initially uncover a series of somehow related goals and thoughts that should be discharged and flattened as we go along.

***III-1. (As the ID) Is there a continuous effect you want to impress on the opponent?**
(As the ID) Is there something that must not happen?
(As the ID) Is there something that you consider as good?
(As the ID) Is there something that you consider as bad?
(As the ID) Is there something you seem to always want or desire?
(As the ID) Is there something you see as highly undesirably?
(As the ID) is there something that is forbidden to do?
(As the ID) Is there something that you consider as your duty?
(As the ID) is there something that makes you happy and fulfilled?
(As the ID) Is there a certain state of affairs you want to bring about?
(In conclusion) what would you say is the character's main goal?

If the initial dialogue has already answered most or all of these questions, it would make sense to ask directly for the main goal. So use the above questions with that in mind.

Any angle that can be discharged with DEEP tools is applied. If you have a clear statement of a goal or thought you would run it with Repeating. Have the character say it once and await acknowledgment. This is done repeatedly until that item is discharged. Also, have the character say it in different moods, starting with a low tone level and moving up, using repeating at each level until discharged. You want to discharge the whole DEEP package, including effort and emotion. So ask for them and discharge what is found. When things settle down the basic goal should be visible. Should the goal become clear at any time, we are done with the step. We recheck the item later in 'Section VII – Confirm the Main Goal.'

Section IV. Attitudes

Once a character is formed it will seek to survive. It will hold on to and boost its ego and self-importance by various means. In this section we are looking for defensive and aggressive attitudes that may be typical for the character. We are also looking for any self-serving computation (SSC) that routinely can be found at the center of such attitudes.

***IV-3. Take the VP of character...**

- **AB-a. (As the ID) is there a typical attitude or automatic reaction you use to defend yourself?**
- **AB-b. (As the ID) is there a typical attitude or automatic reaction you use to gain control?**
- **AB-c. (As the ID) is there a typical attitude or automatic reaction you use to uphold your own importance?**
- **AB-d. (As the ID) is there a typical attitude or automatic reaction you use to get what you want?**

After each AB question answer you can check for how that could be worded: **"Can you formulate that as a rule or self-serving computation that you follow?** If you get one, you run the DEEP package, starting with Repeating. Sometimes you will have to settle for the attitude by itself and run it as an impulse or effort.

You take the wording or the named attitude and run the following:

"How has (SSC/attitude) helped you?" "How has (SSC/attitude) harmed you?" Also (if needed):

"What unwanted situation has it gotten you into?"" What unwanted situation has it gotten you out of?"

Section V. Natural Self

***V-1. Is there a natural side of yourself (the introspector) that has been suppressed, squashed or ignored by [current character]?**

We want an answer that expresses the natural side. Say, "happy Joe", "caring Joe", "responsible Joe", etc. where 'Joe' is the introspector's name and 'happy', 'caring', 'responsible' are given as the natural side suppressed.

*V-2. Run 'Hello-OK' and 'Identities Dialogue' between natural-self and the character.

Do this back and forth until there is no more to be said on both sides.

You may recheck V-1 as there can be more than one side suppressed.

Section VI. Nemesis Pole

There is another typical polarization that should be addressed as a routine. There is typically a person or sinister character our character abhors or fears. This is the character's tormentor or Nemesis. In Greek mythology 'Nemesis' is the goddess of righteous vengeance. Nemesis is used about a character that seems to pursue and haunt somebody. It is a judging character who seems to remind the person of his/her fallibilities and wrong-doings. Finding the nemesis was originally intended to find the opposing side of the main conflict. But often it gave surprising answers that weren't the other side. Still, it is a split that in part defines the main character. The Nemesis is what is haunting our main character or is his worst nightmare.

VI-1. Finding the nemesis pole.
Assume the VP of the character.
"Is there a personal Nemesis or tormentor?
VI-2. Run Hello/OK and dialogue between the two, nemesis and character.

If the answer cannot be personalized (such as "fear" it is flattened with Repeat and Tell and other DEEP tools.)

The Nemesis question is rechecked as there can be more than one item.

Section VII. Confirm the Main Effort/Goal

In section III above we found the main goal. Now we want to confirm it as it is so central to the character.

***VII-1 In the character [name] we found [main effort/goal] to be the main goal.**
Does that still seem to be correct?
If no clear item was found earlier, see if it is available now, possibly referring to and sorting out the earlier answers. If a different wording or effort is found now, make sure to flatten with Repeat and Tell.

Section VIII. Effort Buttons: Fully discharging the character

*VIII-1. Tell the introspector: *"The following are buttons to find efforts or impulses in play in the character. Whatever effort, emotion, impulse or thought a button may trigger is of great interest to the clearer. We want to flatten anything charged that shows up and then recheck the button."*

We mainly use 'Repeat and Tell', but other tools from the tool box can be used as well.

Once we get a response to one of the questions below, we start running it. The introspector may answer with another effort/impulse than the one directly asked for in the question. If so, we take that anyway. "Experience that [effort/impulse]", or "Get that [effort/impulse]" or "show me that effort/impulse" is used repeatedly. Also "Replay that [effort/impulse]" can be used. One can ask into it and other DEEP elements may turn up that need to be flattened in turn. Also, running any opposition or resistance should be done as a routine. *"Do you perceive any opposition or resistance against that?"* can be asked. We then recheck the original question and run it until we have the answer "No" to the original question. Then we move on to the next button.

Example: You ask "...effort or impulse to protect?" The introspector gives 'effort to hold on to my friend.' You run that: "Experience that effort to hold on to your friend." until flat. Then clearer asks again for "...effort or impulse to protect?" The introspector says 'yes, effort to protect my money.' Clearer runs that: "Get (or 'show me') the effort of protecting your money." till flat. On rechecking "...Effort or impulse to protect?" the clearer gets a 'No', and therefore moves on to the next button, 'Defend.'

It can happen that we are getting a 'yes' answer and the same effort is given by the introspector even after having run repeating on it. If so, the first thing to ask for is any opposition ('Is there any opposition to Effort to protect your money?'). If so, run that with Repeat and Tell from the opposition's viewpoint.

One can also go back and forth between opposites. "Get the idea of experiencing [the effort/emotion, etc.]" "Get the idea of not experiencing [the effort/emotion, etc.]"

This method simply gives us another way of looking at the DEEP element and discharges it further.

In general: Usually a DEEP element becomes discharged after a few repeatings. But sometimes it may take 20 or more repeatings before it goes flat. And sometimes it takes other tools to fully discharge the DEEP item including finding the opposition.

The whole character may discharge and blow at some point. This can happen at any point of DCC. If the introspector originates it is gone, or there seems nothing left to run, one would end off that particular session. On such an origination, one would take it as a session end point and recheck at beginning of next session if it was just a temporary highpoint. If it seems to hold, one would move forward and find the other side of the polarity. This may already have been uncovered during the previous running when we have checked for opposition and resistance.

If the character has become discharged to a large extent at the point of the Effort Buttons, we would still check the buttons but would spend less time on the procedure, mainly looking for overlooked charges on both sides of the polarity and only do repeating if it seems productive. We would simply do Effort Buttons in fast forward and just pick up things that had been overlooked.

Effort Buttons

The main question we use is: **"in [character] [with ... [the main goal], is there an effort or impulse to...":**

This question may seem very long. But it is necessary to keep reminding the introspector of the character in question. Therefore we repeat regularly the name of the character and the main goal, the two most defining qualities of the character. If the name or main goal is too long to repeat in the question, we can use another formulation. "We have this character, 'Nervous Sailor, who whistles in stormy weather,' with the main effort 'to check all ropes and sails every 5 minutes'...

In this character, is there an effort or impulse to...?"

Of course, if one is going forward rapidly, due to most of the charge gone, one only has to remind the introspector from time to time. But if the clearer just finished a long run of one button he/she would certainly have to remind the introspector in context with the next button question.

We have one section with Effort Buttons and one section with Tractor Buttons. The Effort Buttons are outgoing efforts that all may be in play in the performance of the character. It is a list of actions that may be needed, a sort of organizing board. You could compare it to all the posts and actions needed if it were a company replacing the character. The Tractor Buttons cover wanted and desired actions and responses the character craves or seeks to evoke from other players.

***VIII-2. Ask, one at a time, "in [character] with [the main goal], is there an effort or impulse to...":**

- ***EB.a. "...protect something or someone?"**
- ***EB.b. "...defend something or someone?"**
- ***EB.c "...attack something or someone?"**
- ***EB.d. "...avoid something or someone?"**
- ***EB.e. "...hide something or someone?"**
- ***EB.f. "...suppress something or someone?"**
- ***EB.g. "...hold on to a state or condition?"**
- ***EB.h. "...get rid of a state or condition?"**
- ***EB.i. "...to make something persist or prevail?"**
- ***EB.j. "...nourish or grow something?"**
- ***EB.k. "...condemn or cut off someone?"**
- ***EB.L. "...conquer something?"**
- ***EB.m. "...to engage someone in an emotional exchange?"**
- ***EB.n. "...dominate something or someone?"**
- ***EB.o. "...make wrong?"**
- ***EB.p. "...stop something or someone?"**
- ***EB.q. "...control or discipline self?"**
- ***EB.r. "...control or discipline others?"**
- ***EB.s. "...of hypnotic (automatic) acceptance of anything coming from a certain source?"**
- ***EB.t. "...to disagree with or fight anything coming from a certain source?"**

You can use these questions from time to time – or at least at the end:
"Is there some effort I haven't asked for that came up?"
"Is there any other effort of an outgoing nature that I have not asked for?"

Other buttons can be used, e.g. buttons originated by the introspector; others can be added by the clearer to adapt to the introspector and situation.

VIII-3. Tractor Buttons

***TBs. Ask, one at the time, "in [character] with [the main goal], is there a craving or desire to...":**

- ***TB.a ... get someone's affection or love?**
- ***TB.b ... get someone's agreement?**
- ***TB.c ... get someone's communication?**

- ***TB.d ... get someone's understanding?**
- ***TB.e ...to experience physical contact or mass?**
- ***TB.f ... get someone's property or money?**
- ***TB.g ... get someone's energy or cooperation?**
- ***TB.h ... get someone's space?**
- ***TB.i ... get someone's time?**
- ***TB.j ... get someone's position (as a job)?**
- ***TB.k ... get someone's anger or disapproval?**
- ***TB.L ... get someone's clear response?**
- ***TB.m ...to exchange sensations or emotions?**
- ***TB.n ... be admired or worshipped?**
- ***TB.o ... to be supported or provided for?**
- ***TB.p ... get someone's help?**
- ***TB.q ... get information or knowhow?**
- ***TB.r ... get someone to evolve or to grow?**
- ***TB.s ... get someone to change?**
- ***TB.t ... make someone or something smaller?**
- ***TB.u ... make someone or something weaker?**
- ***TB.v ... reduce someone or something?**
- ***TB.w ... get someone's body?**
- ***TB.x ... get someone's girlfriend or wife / boyfriend or husband?**
- ***TB.y ... to experience s/o else's pleasure or sensation?**

You can use these questions from time to time – or at least at the end:
"Is there some craving or desire I haven't asked for that came up?"
"Is there any other craving or desire I haven't asked for?"

Other buttons can be used, e.g. buttons originated by the introspector. Others can be added by the clearer to adapt to the introspector and situation.

Section IX. Final Step on Character

Finally, do a Hello/OK and dialogue between the introspector and the character if needed.
Also 6 Directions on the character is a usable last step.

This completes the running of the character.

Section X. Finding the Other Pole

A true pole/counter-pole situation generates an eternal charge and is an unsolvable problem. The two sides are in a games condition fighting each other and the conflict just goes on and on. The one pole agonizes and has endless problems with the other pole and vice versa— besides: they usually have their attention fixated on the opposite pole. "Fighting the good fight" is all they can think of.

Such a fight to the death or destruction of the other is not always what we find—and thank you for that! But in DCC, when looking for the opposite pole, we always look for such a situation so we catch it if it's there.

We started the running of DCC with a counter-pole, a known individual the introspector has had endless troubles with. So the pole we now are looking for will, in some form, be the introspector him or herself. It isn't enough, however, to call the pole for 'Jim' if that is the introspector's name. It is important to nail the person's state of mind in this conflict. It could be, 'Jim, the troublemaker,' 'Jim, the outrageous,' etc.

So first the clearer will discuss the conflicts the introspector, Jim, has had with his counter-pole, say, his father. What do all these conflicts have in common?

What is the role Jim is prone to slip into, to dramatize? Jim, the defender? the liberator? the rebellion? the brilliant? the reformer? the superior? or what?

The clearer sorts out with the introspector, sometimes at length, the possible role the introspector dramatizes in these fights.

Also the clearer should check that the role the introspector slips into in these fights is a major problem to the counter-pole, the father, to the other character we have just run. As an example, one would ask if 'Jim, the Brilliant' would be a real problem to 'Father, the General.'

In the example, we would have a 'general' who mainly wants order, discipline and compliance; and a son who mainly wants to discuss things, have applause for his wit, do new things, etc. You see? An unsolvable problem or constellation.

The procedure goes like this:
***X-1. The clearer asks: In dealing with counter-pole ("Father, the General") what kinds of conflicts would often take place?**

This is discussed in order to uncover the behavioral patterns of both parties.

We are focusing on the introspector's behavior, of course.

***X-2. Clearer asks into what the introspector's active role is in the conflict and finds the role. The role the introspector dramatizes.**

If the clearer has run the other side properly, going back and forth between counter-pole and the introspector's own reactions and views, this identity should be easily visible.

Sometimes, however, it may take some time to find the introspector's actual role in the conflict. The introspector may claim to be the innocent victim for a while.

But really, what is needed is to find a role that somehow agonizes the counter-pole and thus keeps the conflict going.

It can be a help sometimes to run this formal technique:
Recall a conflict with [counter-pole]
Was there some role you dramatized?
What was your active role in that conflict?

This is run repetitively until the introspector cognites on the common denominator and own role in the relationship.

Note: There is the possibility that the one side dominates and the other side is mainly trying to avoid direct confrontation. This is often the case with a child><parent conflict where the parent is seen as the all-dominant authority figure. The child in such a conflict is just trying to survive long enough and then move away from the childhood home. In such case, get the counter-pole (the child in example) formulated as being a problem to the pole just run (parent pole) and then run that character. In the example it could be 'needy child', 'noisy child', etc. It is not a head to head conflict but still a long and charged one that is well suited for DCC.

***X-3. Clearer makes sure the role now established is a problem to the just run counter-pole.**

Once you have a candidate (say, Jim the Brilliant) check to see if this could agonize the other side (Father, the General.)

You compare with some of the conflicts discussed with the introspector earlier to see if it matches up.

When it does, you have found the other pole, the other character in the conflict.

This role is now taken through the DCC steps above.

Chapter 15: GPM Series 9
Applications of DEEP Character Clearing

Note: *This chapter gives some important data on DEEP Character Clearing, our flag ship procedure. Furthermore, It gives an outline for handling typical issues that persons have, such as relationship problems, etc. Such a mini-program is called an Application. Just like you can get applications or app's to your mobile phone, clearers here have Applications designed to handle typical issues that clients present in session. An overall plan for case handling, covering many sessions, is called a program. It is usually made up at the beginning of clearing work based on an in depth interview of the client.*

What we address in DEEP Character Clearing is first and foremost identities. What we are interested in is emotionally charged identities the person has been and identities the person has fought. These identities, in other words, would include own identities and any identity the person has had some kind of problematic relationship with, present and past.

An identity is a set way of going about handling things. It has its strengths by 'knowing exactly what to do', by having become 'second nature' to its owner. It's a convenience and an automaticity. We go to school to get an education in order to form the more useful identities. We copy and learn from our parents and from other role models to get ahead in life. Some of this is useful, some of it is harmful. There are, however, outright reactive or negative identities we hold on to for dear life. Many of them are a mix of traits that can be useful under certain circumstances but there are routinely also irrational or reactive traits. Identities have their weakness in terms of having been formed in the past and may respond to past situations rather than the present one. In other words, they may operate on old or faulty data and in an obsessive manner. In a sense, these IDs are "the bureaucrats of the mind". Like a bureaucrat-function is set up by a top boss at some point to resolve a specific set of circumstances and follow a well-defined job-description and function, the IDs of the mind are set up by the person him/ herself to resolve or respond to specific situations and circumstances. In a bureaucracy, the only entity, the only "bureaucrat", that is stably at cause, is the top boss who can change the rules of the game. He/she can change the job descriptions, the hats, the functions and routines. DEEP Character Clearing has as its aim to enable the client to become this top boss in relation to his own roles and games in life. The client can review and revise all these personal 'bureaucrats of the mind' with their automaticities and set patterns that in some cases have become the masters rather than the servants.

Each ID of the mind operates on a goal that is somewhat obsessive. An ID also operates on purposes and policies, which perhaps are better described as 'now I am supposed to's' in terms of what to do, and on 'beliefs' which are firm rules and convictions that work as the IDs policies. Much of the data an ID of the mind is operating on has traumatic underpinnings. The ID identifies dangers of past situations with things that are similar in present time, but harmless. So danger and fear is assigned to a lot of harmless things this way. Rules and behaviors that only made sense in emergency situations are held as firm beliefs and universal laws. They have become self-limiting and self-destructive.

Why Concentrate on IDs?

There are other techniques within the clearing tech family, not part of DEEP, that exclusively concentrate on running the goals that formed the IDs. It is true that the goal is the live and continued intention that forms an ID. A young man may have the goal to fight crime and work for justice. To live his goal, our man becomes a police officer. Our young man is a very dedicated police officer who goes to work every morning full of energy and determination. Our police man will run into all kinds of dramatic situations and experiences while doing his job. Gradually, from being a young, idealistic police cadet, our officer becomes a hardened, no nonsense veteran, unwilling to listen to anyone's excuses and explanations, unwilling to take even colleagues' advice. Our police officer has become a hardened cop ID. His job performance has become a petrified routine dominated by effort. It has been cast in concrete, so to speak. In theory, just running the goal and get the emotional charge off it, should handle it all. But in practical clearing work it soon becomes clear that the ID is the container that holds all the emotional charge. There is a lot of mental mass in these goal-identity-super-problems. And the mass is not the live intentions. It is the residue they leave behind, the identities. We can maybe get our police man to change his mind and get some of his original enthusiasm back by running the goal only. But there is still a lot of reactive luggage that isn't taken care of. We have to take care of the mental mass. It all sits in the ID.

The relationship between goals and IDs can also be understood as that of a game and the players. The game defines the goal. A game is an overall objective and a set of rules. It does not contain mass nor can the game itself become a casualty. The players are shaped by the game. Players get injured, upset, overwhelmed, etc. while playing. They accumulate experiences and mental mass. The game of the police man is to fight crime. The officers are formed by what the police work requires of them. In DEEP Character Clearing we deal first and foremost in rehabilitating the player or players and then in getting a better grasp of the game. So in DCC we spend a lot of time on dealing directly with the ID. Once the emotional charge of the ID is handled, our police officer will be in a state of mind where he can re-energize his goal to fight crime and work for justice – or he is free to change his mind about his police career. He is no longer stuck in the obsessive role of a nasty cop. He is no longer stuck in an obsessive game.

Another way to illustrate the importance of IDs compared to goals is to compare an ID with an old dwelling the spiritual Being lives in. Let's say, it started out with a piece of land and a simple summer cottage. Over time the cottage was added to and improved. At some point it has become a real house, fitted to withstand severe conditions, like rains, storms, cold weather and flooding. Electricity is installed and at some point the electric wiring had to be redone to align with a new building code. A better roof is put on. A new porch and a workshop are added. The workshop is turned into living space and walls are, at some point, put up to make separate rooms for the children. They are taken down again when the kids leave home as the mistress of the house now wants an atelier as she has taken up painting. So we live in houses of our own doing, if not entirely of our own making. Life can be awfully complicated in a house like that as it was built piecemeal. Still, living in this house we get so used to it that we forget about its poor functionality. Its dripping faucets, the door that won't close, the smoking furnace, the leaking roof, the squeaky floorboard, etc. It takes a lot of work, obviously, to get such a house into shape and suitable for comfortable living. There are many details to see to. It cannot, in our experience, be done with a magic wand. You cannot just wave a magic wand and say, "the goal is a comfortable home, a place we can live in and operate from." We have to invest the work necessary to bring that about. It takes some hard work to fulfill the goal of the place: a comfortable home we can live in and operate from. Likewise with IDs. There are many nooks and crannies that have to be inspected, reevaluated and changed in order for the ID to be up to speed and 'current building code', if you will. Now the goal can be made to shine as with a magical wand. The game will be enjoyable and under the person's control.

IDs as Pairs

Irrational IDs that are in restimulation will often be found in pairs. The most charged IDs are found to be two live IDs in the person's mind that seem to fight each other. 'Cop vs Robbers' may be our police officer's biggest problem. It is what we call an obsessive games-condition. He both holds and energizes his own role as cop but also the role of the robber, the criminal. This is a surprising fact, but an important one. Maybe he formed this ID of the criminal to be fully prepared for his job, being able to predict the opponent's next move. There are other theories.

The two sides are, however, somehow locked together in an obsessive games-condition. The one side triggers the other and vice versa. They are on some kind of collision course, in some kind of charged relationship. You see the one ID is set up to deal with the other side, the opponent. A woman, let's say, is dealing with 'a tyrannical boss' by forming 'a submissive and charming employee' as an ID. Both the boss ID and the woman employee ID can be found as IDs in the woman's mental make-up. Over time, these IDs develop a complex pattern of responses to each other. One will find a great number of related IDs that are operating within the same sphere of interest or specialized game within life. An example of such a game could be 'marriage'. There are dozens of roles related to marriage that a person can get stuck in. Not only countless variations of husband and wife; there are numerous supporting roles, such as mother-in-law's, siblings, children, extra marital lovers/mistresses, hotel owners, landlords, etc., etc. It covers all the plots that movies and novels describe and entertain us with. One will find IDs within the 'game of marriage' that are in all sorts of games-conditions with each other and that these games and scenarios repeat themselves over and over. Another example of such a game is politics. Again, you see patterns repeat themselves over and over. The politicians may appear to be actors on a stage having to follow an old script. Other well-known games are the corporate career game, a certain profession (say, farmer and farming), sales with a buyer and a seller, war with an army and an enemy army, etc., etc.

Applications

In practical clearing work we use a number of DEEP techniques to handle basic issues. DEEP Character Clearing remains the flag ship. But as in any other endeavor in life, many good efforts and tools have to be brought together to ensure success. The following outlines the original use of DCC only and some alternative applications, primarily intended for less experienced clients. But they may also be of use with more experienced clients if DCC alone is not really 'biting' on the issue at hand as it should.

To get started on finding irrational identities, we can simply have the client look at his/her present life. The first action is usually to look at relationships, then conditions, then unwanted traits and addictions. One can then look at the person's attitude to different environments, be it work, family, scary environments, etc. Finally one can take up eternal themes. The themes are games in life that have been played for times immemorial as mentioned above: marriage, politics, corporate career, farming, sales, cops and robbers, war, etc.

Troubled Relationships

With Experienced Clients: The clearer finds troubled relationships, past and present, in the client's life. The key question is **"Who have you had troubles with?"** The clearer makes a list and sorts the items by charge. The most charged counter-pole is taken through the DCC procedure explained in a previous chapter. The emotional charge is removed step by step so the client eventually fully resolves the obsessive nature of the item. It becomes clearly separate from self and from the opponent's physical person as well. Once the counter-pole side is taken to its End Point, the clearer finds the Own ID that was being triggered in the relationship and it is given a similar discharge to its End Point. How to find the client's own role in the conflict is explained in more detail in the DCC procedure.

Assessing for the Item, with or without Biomonitor

The clearer may use a biomonitor or meter. The item that gives the biggest reaction or longest "read" on the biomonitor is the most charged. The clearer watches the instrument while the client first answers with the item. Or the clearer may have to read back the finished list to find the item with the most reaction. An item that reacts well is hot. It is not only charged, it is also accessible. The client will have a lot to say about it. The clearer then takes up this the most charged item.

Finding the item can also be done without the use of a biomonitor. The clearer has the list of items. The clearer then rates each item for charge by asking, "on a scale from 0-10, 0 being no charge, 10 being maximum charge, how would you rate item 1?" Then item 2, 3, etc. If 2 items both are rated 10, let's say, the item with the longest history is preferred. An item like 'mother' has a much longer history than a co-worker, for instance. There is a childhood full of experiences with 'mother' and only two years, 9-5, with the co-worker. The clearer can also ask which of the two items has the greatest interest to the client to break a tie. Interest is always an important factor. It ensures the client's engagement which is key to excellent results.

Conditions

Once troubled relationships are well in hand, we start to focus on conditions. This is a broad category and mainly anything that is an answer to **"What have you had troubles with?"** The clearer isolates the troubles the person has experienced into traits, feelings, etc. that can be ascribed to an ID. And if this is successful, the ID and its triggered opposition ID can be processed in a similar manner as in relationships. We can get IDs as 'a timid person' 'an overworked person' and the like. These are descriptions of the client's own state of mind in the area of interest. The clearer then runs this the person's own ID though the DCC procedure. Once the 'timid person' is handled the counter-pole of a 'dominating father' may turn up and is run with DCC.

The clearer can also take another approach using the various methods of DEEP. Often there isn't a clear cut ID that offers itself. If the person had troubles with a certain group or a certain activity it would most likely be better to use other DEEP techniques first, that would yield a fuller picture. Let's say, the client has problems with public speaking. A good, workable approach is the following. 1.

Interview the person to find out exactly what the problem is and get data about the circumstances. There may be distinct incidents; there may be certain audiences or subjects; there may be too much going on and the person is confused and cannot isolate or clearly see what he/she does wrong, thinks and feels in the situations. 2. You can take the whole subject of 'public speaking and do a DEEP Subject Clearing on it. Emotional charge will come off and maybe the client now can see what IDs are in play. If not, distinct traumatic incidents may have surfaced. These incidents can be taken up with DEEP Incident Clearing or with DEEP Viewpoint Clearing. They can also be made subject to a more detailed DEEP Subject Clearing session, where the subject taken up is the incident itself. It is preferable to use DEEP Incident Clearing on less experienced clients and DEEP Viewpoint Clearing on experienced clients. These two procedures, DIC and DVC, have as a part of the procedure to run points of view and the whole puzzle with what IDs and characters are in play begins to unravel. From all this one or two resistive characters may stand out and they can now be taken up with DCC.

Another way into trouble areas is to find a relevant goal and do some repeating on that and it turns on an energy-mass. Example: I wanted to run charge off marriage and romantic relationships in general on a client. We started with the goal "to have a sexual relationship". It turned on masses around the head which got labeled, "enraged husband." The main effort of that ID was found to be "to punish the 'sinner' (the woman)." All the steps were run but these are the defining items found (character and goal).

Unwanted Traits and Addictions

"I hate myself for being... (say, lazy)" is heard often enough. Obviously there is an internal conflict among IDs going on or the person would simply l-o-v-e to do nothing and relax all the time. Again, we can find two opposing IDs and use DCC to bring about a more optimum state. Addiction to substances (drugs, food, smoking, etc.) and activities (games, computers, TV, sex, gambling, etc.) can be addressed with DCC as the addicted personality is in conflict with the same person's better side. As of yet, this has not been attempted using DCC but we are optimistic that we can produce good results with an adapted approach.

Note on running smoking: started with the goal "to smoke" it turned on a distinct energy-mass. When it was developed I gave it a temporary ID label, "smoker joker". Later, at the step "in terms of beingness or being, what shall we call this character", it was found to be, "a demonstrated independent individual". Later again the main effort (goal) was found to be, "to remain independent." In this case smoking could possibly be understood as an attribute to this character. The best approach to addictions is not DCC however. We are developing a high-powered action under the title DEEP Body Clearing Pro that addresses the body side very well.

Environments

It can be said that the sum total of a human's personality is the accumulated result of 'safe solutions'. The person has worked out hats for all the situations she is exposed to. A hat could be defined as a rational ID. It is, however, also a fact that much of what a human uses and acts on are irrational data and routines. Some of these 'safe' solutions are not safe at all or have serious consequences. An example would be 'shoot first, ask questions later' as part of an ID for a police man. The key question to process Safe Solutions to Environments is: "In terms of attitude or way of being, what would be a safe solution to [general or a specified] environment?"

This approach will expose some core beliefs and attitudes that can be ascribed to an ID. The person can then examine the area for herself and revise as needed.

Dramatizations

In a process known as R6EW, one starts out by finding what the client is dramatizing (unknowingly acting out). It is something caused by the person's reactive or unconscious mind rather than a reaction to something in the present. We use a technique inspired by that. One looks over one's case and perceives something irrational and unwanted. One names it very briefly, preferably with only one word, such as nervousness, immobility, etc. By repeating the word or short expression used as label one can develop the relevant masses and get into DEEP that way. This technique is very broad as one can always find something to run.

Themes (Eternal Games)

Ron Hubbard developed a concept called End-words. An End-word is a common denominator for a GPM. GPM means Goals-Problems-Mass. At its core, it consists of goals in conflict. Each goal is held by what we call an ID. The goals and the goals-conflicts change and decay over time and form a pattern called line-plots. Each GPM, however, is held together by a theme, a certain game, such as cops and robbers, marriage, etc. as described above. The 'name of the game' can be summed up in what is called an End-word (say, 'Marriage'). An example of opposing goals could be 'to want marriage'>< 'to reject marriage' (both goals have the End-word 'marriage'). The conflict accumulates charge and is eventually given up. But a basic theme, such as marriage, is never really given up on. It may be put on hold even for several lifetimes but the impulse and desire never die. Thus it is in play over and over and will accumulate many other conflicts that will be piled on top of the existing ones. Over eons of time, we get a super-problem — a GPM.

DCC can be used to address these games of life as almost eternal activities. The point is, these games are so basic to being in this universe, and ultimate victory is so attractive so we just never have given up on them. Since we have played them "forever" they have accumulated lots of mental mass and aberration. Some games may be repulsive rather than attractive, but they have so much power over us so we have been hooked on them for a long, long time — enough to accumulate the GPM charge.

Failed Goals 2010

You ask: **"What goal have you worked hard at without really succeeding?"** or a similar question. Once you have the failed goal you do repeating on that and you find the masses, etc. related to that and you are into the procedure. There will be a twist to how the person goes about it. It may be an irrational Modus Operandi (computation), it may be that the goal itself has a twist to it and it may be all kinds of other factors kicking in.

Goals Matrix 2010

You have a prepared list of typical goals. Many of these goals can be found on OT2 platens (prepared lists). In the OT2 incident they were messed up by using implant techniques, but the goals themselves are very basic goals in this universe (and many in the spiritual universe) and they existed long time before any implanting took place. They outline the games played in this universe and you see them paly out again and again in stories and movies. Examples: to have a family; to get rich; to rule as a king; to succeed in ....; to dazzle people; to seduce (opposite sex); to create knowledge; to rule the world, etc., etc.

You take a goal from the list that is charged and do repeating on it. From there you find the masses and energies it triggers and you are into the DEEP procedure.

Masses and Energies 2010

Another way to run DEEP is to notice masses and energies in one's personal space which don't seem to belong there or seem to be irrational.

One starts with developing the masses etc. by "making them more solid" etc. and once one has worked on this for a while, the masses can be identified in terms of character and goal and you run DEEP from there. This method is less reliable as masses and energies usually is the result of two IDs colliding and if one cannot separate out the one from the other, it will not offer an inroad.

Running of DCC

DCC runs best with experienced clients. For new clients there are many other processes and techniques that will help resolve immediate issues, situations and problems. At some point the person will, however, be ready for DCC and once that is the case it offers a technique that will terminatedly take care of even very resistive issues.

A brief outline of how the process works is the following, using the Relationships Process as example: we start with an issue, say, a troubled relationship with the boss, Mr. Jones. The client will typically have a history of the kind of troubles addressed, dating back to other bosses and similar authoritative relationships. First we find a general wording for the type of ID the client is up against. It often has an archetypical ring to it. "An authoritative boss" will do here. From there, we can find an energy ridge of clear size and impact that corresponds to 'boss'. It will usually reside in or around the body and is of the client's own making we assume, as that is how it is addressed successfully. Once the size and impact of this energy ridge is established, we treat it as an entity separate from the client. We can discharge it for emotional content. We find the goals, purposes and beliefs it operates on and include in the mix fixed ideas of making self right and others wrong. Each idea found is initially addressed with Repeater technique. Repeater technique consists of repeating the statement to bleed the charge off. We have however come up with a refinement that makes it work faster and cleaner. At some point the initial charge is gone. But who knows? The release may just last until the client has a situation with the boss once more. Therefore, the postulates that were keyed out, using Repeater technique, need to be traced back to their engramic underpinnings. Some of these postulates are very aberrated and don't just go "poof". If there initially were 12 postulates, including the basic goal it operates on, that made up the mode of operation of the identity, it will be found that a few of those are still heavily charged. One would assume it would be the goal, but that is not always the case. The approach is to discharge the postulates that still have charge and that will take care of the goal. The goal was the starting point of the formation of the ID but it is not necessarily where the ID is really hung up after it has been used or been fought for times immemorial. We trace the charged postulates back to when they were heavily in play or, ideally, to when they were first formed. Here we have several techniques, all under the heading of incident recalling and running, that are very effective. The underpinnings we find are not always engrams or severe physical trauma — although sometimes they are. What we find at the core of what made these postulates stick, are moments of confusion and overwhelm. In terms of engram running, this is a high powered lock. Since we are looking for postulates and decisions rather than physical pain, finding these moments and discharging them is very effective. "The person was in shock and made a stupid decision", is pretty much the common denominator.

Once the energy ridge representing the boss is discharged, we are only half way. It is time to find the role the client has used through his working career to fight or handle a boss with. That is the other side of the equation that is overlooked in most processing. There is an internal battle going on between 'boss' and 'employee' in this case. One has to discharge both sides to fully move out of the fixed situations and the dramatizations contained therein. The discharge of the client's own 'favorite role' when it comes to handling difficult bosses is processed in a similar fashion as described above.

There are many ways to find initial troublesome identities and that is exploited in the different headline actions described above.

Philosophical Model

The model this processing builds on is quite simple, although maybe controversial to some. What motivates and animates a human being is the Spirit or Thetan. In its native state it's a Static. According to Scientology Axiom One: Life is basically a static. Definition: a Life Static has no mass, no motion, no wavelength, no location in space or in time. It has the ability to postulate and to perceive.

One of the first actions of the Static, after a decision to participate in a certain activity, is to assume a point of view, the beginnings of an ID. But the point of view is still under the Static's full control. The fact is, to play any game in the physical universe, and most other universes, the first action is to assume a stable position, a point of view.

When we look at a human being as we exist today, we are looking at a composite. Traditionally we have spirit-mind-body. To this classic triumvirate one could add Identity. In our model, it would be Spirit- Identity-Mind-Body. One could even say: Spirit-Identities-Minds-Body. Even though a human being usually is remarkably well coordinated, one can find many IDs within her and each has 'a mind of its own' to some extent.

What we do in our Processing, is to locate these stuck points of view. Each has a basic goal it developed from. It has accumulated experiences, conclusions, purposes and policies it operates on. Each ID is a state of mind that built up around being in that game for a long, long time. The goal and its ID were assumed at some point in the past. They became "the appointed bureaucrats of the Static" empowered completely to take care of a very specific goal and set of circumstances. Through DCC processing, the person, once more, gains full control over that ID to a point where it's no more an obsessive role the Being slips into. We can help the client overcome 'bureaucratic infightings" and all kinds of irrational thinking and behavior.

The ultimate goal of DCC processing would be to restore the spirit, once more, to its native state of a Static. Since the processing is an activity requiring a point of view, one has to do it by pulling the person up by the bootstraps, so to speak. It will not all happen in a short period of time. Fortunately, we have some very desirable states of personal improvement to offer during the journey, as described above under the different actions DCC consists of.

Chapter 16
DEEP Space Clearing (DSPC)

by Heidrun Beer

If you are a lover of Science Fiction, you certainly remember the expression "Space-Time-Continuum" that has been coined by mathematician Hermann Minkowski in 1906, soon after Albert Einstein defined his special theory of relativity. It was used by Science Fiction authors to describe their hyperspace travel adventures.

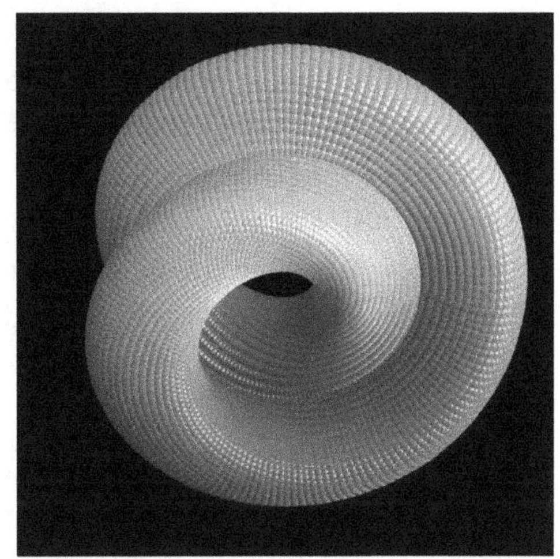

Today it is also called "Spacetime". Wikipedia writes:

> **In physics, spacetime is any mathematical model which fuses the three dimensions of space and the one dimension of time into a single four-dimensional manifold.**

We will not get more into the theory of this or its many opportunities to make intriguing pictures. What interests us is a novel view of our client's case (and of course our own). All we need to remember of the theory is really that space and time are intimately fused, that one never exists without the other. And since our case consists of recordings of existence, space and time are equally fused in these recordings.

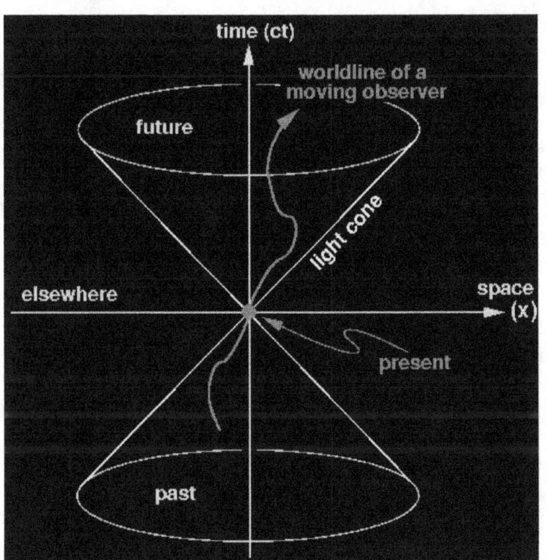

In other words: A point on the timeline always corresponds with one location in space - while a location in space can correspond with many points on the timeline, which makes it a great asset in accessing a lot of charge in one swoop. Especially for clients who have done a lot of sessions and have become faster in releasing charge this can be very accommodating. New clients on the other hand may need the more precise timeline-oriented access. As always, it will be a judgment call for the clearer what to use when.

Even in our early training there was a rule that as soon as a client can see the environment (the space) of an incident, he has also located it on the timeline. What we want is always the incident as such, where opposing forces have locked up and captured life-force that we want to un-stick, un-freeze if you like. Traditionally we used to get to the charge by scanning the client's timeline, which then revealed the location (space); with DEEP Space Clearing we get to it by scanning the client's space, which then reveals the charged moments in time having to do with this space.

Any good housewife knows that in order to clean a surface, she must wipe not only from left to right but also up and down. Extrapolating that to the spacetime concept, it would make sense that after a while of cleaning up charge along the client's timeline it could be wise to make a 90° change in direction and do some more work by looking for sparks of charge that light up when his attention touches a certain area in his space.

Remember, space and time are always connected, they are inseparable. We just change the approach, so we have a chance to pick up things that may have been missed before. No matter which way we scan, we always end up with a chunk of charge that is tied to points in BOTH TIME AND SPACE. The principle is a little similar to DEEP Aspect Clearing, but there we scan a space inside the body, and in DEEP Space Clearing it is the client's surrounding space that we scan.

To be totally technically accurate, it is of course the client's mental copy of his outer space where the charge is stored, so the actual location of it would be inside his biofield (the aura or energy body) - but scanning the actual physical space is a great way to access that, at least if his case is structured like the one we describe below, since the sensation of charge is projected to the location where it originated, just like we project the images that are formed in our eye's retina out into our environment. Our brain is used to doing it with visual images all day long, so it is natural to do the same trick with the recordings of charged points in spacetime.

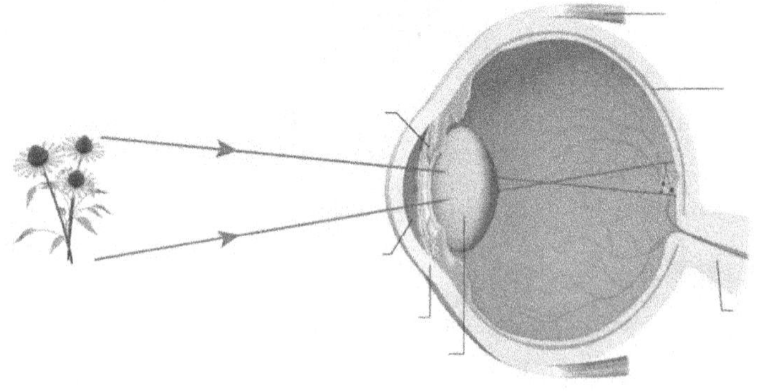

It is therefore entirely a question of perception where the client's charge seems to be located. In some moment of distress, in some defensive or protective move our client has stored his charge at specific coordinates inside his mental copy of the surrounding space, and it is our job to find it exactly where he has placed it, so it can be processed. In other words, it has not only a label with date and time, but also a location label, like a table or chair in a furniture market's display that tells you its aisle and shelf number.

HISTORY

Actually the whole idea to the DEEP Space Clearing approach came from one of our clients' case, which appeared to have a fabric different from the more typical case, where charge is arranged along the timeline (the 4th dimension of spacetime).

In her case, charge was clearly mapped against her 3-dimensional physical space, or rather the different spaces that composed her overall space. From more general areas like countries, cities or buildings it went down to smaller spaces like rooms, a shelf in a room, or even individual boxes on individual shelf boards in a room. A charged school building made her avoid a whole district in her home town. Specific folders had a repelling quality that made her unable to reach for them and work with their content - really bad for her work when it came to writing up the service hours that she needed to send out invoices that would ultimately pay for her livelihood!

Dusty desk corners, wilted indoor plants, moth infested food containers, the clothes of her late husband or old family jewellery - they looked like plain objects to our unaided eye, but for her each of them was really a "space capsule" that was not only telling a story (timeline!) but also holding significant charge. Using these as DEEP items cracked her case - when we were finished, she was on a win for months and completely transformed and upgraded her whole environment (space!).

It was not the emotional pain alone that caused the trouble. Each of these spaces had an ACTION QUALITY to it. Some spaces repelled her so that she was unable to reach them, resulting in a more and more messy appearance of her rooms over time. Other spaces - her bed to some degree, but most importantly her reclining chair with the computer in front of it - held her captive. She often called herself a workaholic, but actually it was her chair that she could not escape. She spent days, weeks and months there, neglecting exercise, neglecting essential household duties, always feeling bad about it but never being able to break out of that "inner prison".

Observing these spaces' apparent actions brought us to an old tool we knew from our earlier training, where a whole list of space related action words was read out to the client in another context. The old drill combined with our new observations revealed the way to go:

KEY PRINCIPLES

In DEEP Space Clearing, we scan a client's space for charged elements, rate them for charge with the method described in the "DEEP Clearing" book – on a scale from 0 to 10, how charged does it feel? – and first of all find the ACTION that the space seems to perform.

Special attention has to be paid to how we ask for this action. We do not want to imply that the spaces that surround our client are somehow after him, that they have some kind of evil intention. Both we and the client (if we educated him well) are aware that any space as such is neutral, that it just acts as an item finder, a pointer to the client's own energies – energies that are aligned to an inner map of the outer space, but not actually located in that outer space.

For example, we would not ask "What is that shelf board doing to you?", but "How does that shelf board seem to act toward you?" or "What action do you perceive coming at you from that shelf board?" In some way or other, our question must always reflect that it is a subjectively perceived action that we ask for, not one that we want to attribute to an actual area in space, as if it had suddenly and mysteriously come alive in a hostile way.

It is not necessary to remind the client of these facts after they have been explained once, or correct him when his answers are not totally technically accurate. We just make sure not to use words that could act as a suggestion (an incorrect one), and that we get valid action words as an answer.

"It seems to PIN me to the chair", "It REPELS me", "It HOLDS ME AWAY so I cannot get to it", "It HOLDS ME INSIDE so I cannot get out of it", "It CHAINS ME DOWN" would be some examples for valid action words, even if they are not all technically accurate. "I cannot get out of the chair" is not a valid action word – if we get such an answer, we need to follow up with something like "OK, and what is it that the chair seems to be doing?" Only with that action precisely perceived as coming from the space in question, can the client later come up with his own counter-action.

If the client cannot really define it but we see what it could be, we can make a suggestion and ask if that is correct (not just assert it). We can even pull out that old list and read it out to the client, but typically going through his space with him – physically or mentally -, pointing at charged sub-spaces and asking for the action they seem to perform is giving us perfect material to address.

In DEEP terms, we now have defined that space as a "counter-pole" to the client. From here on out, it is standard DEEP procedure that we run. All DEEP principles that have been described in the book "DEEP Clearing" apply, and all tools can be used.

We first have the client discharge the impact of the space's apparent ACTION (that we just found) with "Repeat and Tell", and then comes the all-important question "How do you react to that?", which leads us to the client's own DEEP Package, consisting of his counter-action together with the connected emotion and finally the self-limiting thoughts that made the whole package into a life problem for him.

Our model client for instance was struggling with an enormous effort to FOCUS on papers that were REPELLING her. She felt that she had to SQUEEZE her brain to make it work, and since she was not aware of it before we uncovered this effort in session, she never stopped doing it, even when she was off work or sleeping or dreaming. This exhausted her to a point of DESPAIR (the connected emotion). And "I cannot do admin" would be a really life wrecking decision, don't you agree? That is only one of many devastating DEEP Packages that we found in this actual client's case.

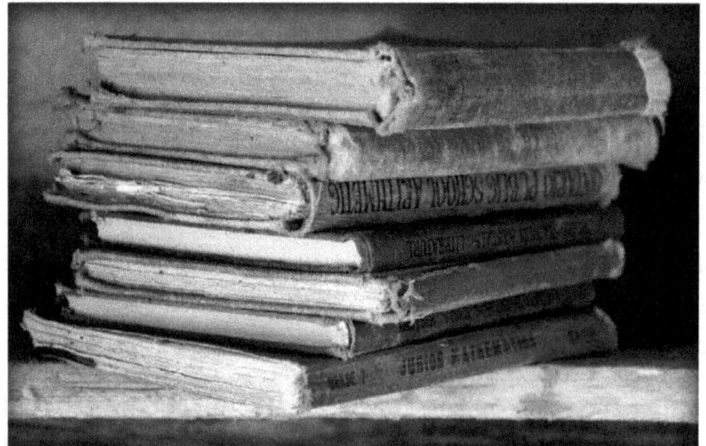

As always when we run DEEP, one thing can lead to another. The innocent looking small space of an old school book can reveal study trouble that we need to run in later sessions with "DEEP Subject Clearing". The beloved deceased family member's jewelry or clothes may reveal losses that have not been addressed before and we will follow up with "DEEP Incident Clearing". "DEEP Character Clearing" may be needed when we uncover a deep-seated old hatred, and so on – in one word, DEEP Space Clearing is not always a standalone procedure, it connects to other DEEP procedures and tools as needed, each in their own well-prepared context (no wild jumping), so that every DEEP element found is fully discharged and nothing is left "dangling".

LIST OF ACTION QUESTIONS

As a general rule, we always prefer that our client finds his own words for what he perceives in his case. It is this act of looking and describing which sharpens his perceptions and over time turns him into what we call a "trained client". This repeated perception training can spill over into life and enable him to become more and more mindful of himself (and others) while he is interacting with family, work mates etc. – not just deal with things in hindsight.

But for new clients who are still in the process of learning how to observe their inner universe, and in situations where the charge is overwhelming or confusing and the client finds it difficult to look at it, it can be helpful to assist with suggestions. We do this only when the client is not able to clearly describe what is happening with him and the space in question, but the charge is there and the space is causing him trouble in life.

Some action words that have worked in the past are compiled in the following list. It is important to always formulate them clearly as a question – we are never, ever trying to tell our client what's happening for him.

The expression **[space]** means that at this point in the question we insert the name of the space that the client has found to be charged – the one we are currently working on.

Did you go into [space]?
Have you previously gone into [space]?
Did somebody place you in [space]?
Have you become stuck in [space]?
Do you want to go into [space]?
Are you unable to get into [space]?
Does [space] seem to repel you (throw you out)?
Do you feel you cannot go into [space]?
Do you feel trapped in [space]?
Have you been forced into [space]?
Do you feel sucked into [space]?
Do you feel pushed into [space]?

This list can of course be expanded, if you find other action questions that work for you and/or a specific client.

If the answer is "yes" to one of these questions, we can immediately work with it. If the answer is "yes" to more than one, we need to find out which has the most charge, work with that, and check the other answers later.

As a rule, we want the client to perceive what action the space seems to be performing. So if he said "yes" to "Do you feel trapped in your bed?", we follow up with "OK, and what is it that your bed seems to be doing?" Let's assume he says "it holds me down like a giant magnet", that's the force whose impact we discharge first, followed by the client's counter-reaction, which is a violent struggle against the giant magnet, combined with matching emotions and thoughts. Standard DEEP principles apply. We can even have the client take the viewpoint of the bed to act out the giant magnet's forceful grip on the helpless human (not a necessity but can be a powerful tool).

On the other hand, some of the questions above can produce an action by the client directly which has lively charge, while the space does not seem to do anything but resist. In that case we can skip the question for the space's action, but while we run the client's action, we add the instruction "spot the [space]'s resistance". An example would be "I so want to get into that corner so I can sort it out". "OK, and what does the corner seem to be doing?" "Nothing, it just doesn't let me in." "Good, now show me your strong reach for that corner (act it out), and while you are doing that, spot its resistance." That would be the entrance to a complete DEEP Package. When that is done, we can again run the corner's viewpoint if running the client's viewpoint does not bring about a real release.

AMPLIFIERS

Like in all session situations, there is sometimes an entity that amplifies some of the forces involved (an invisible but tangible energy form that appears not to be the client's own energy, but makes the client's energy stronger and more resistive). Other amplifiers can be family members or some cultural point of view (morphic field or group mind). They typically discharge nicely when taken up as separate viewpoints. We teach about these invisible energy forms thoroughly in our DEEP training, level 3 (Advanced).

ADDITIONAL FLOWS

If the charge on a space does not fully resolve, it is worth the time to check on the other flows having to do with the same space. If the client caused something harmful or unwanted to another person related to that space, if he observed something painful done between other people related to that space, or if he did something to himself, there would be additional DEEP packages to run. In that case it is important that the space plays a role in the drama: Somebody strangled in a room does not ask for DEEP Space Clearing, it runs as a traumatic incident. Somebody locked up in that same room fits the pattern of DEEP Space Clearing. There must be an action performed by the space itself or against the space itself.

To recapitulate the flow patterns:
Flow 1 – the client is effect of the action
Flow 2 – the client is causing the action
Flow 3 – the client observes an action happening between others
Flow 4 – the client acts on himself

DEEP SPACE CLEARING STEP BY STEP (PROCEDURE)

1. **Find a charged space to work with – originated by client or discovered by scanning the client's environment. Make sure to include spaces that may be outside the client's awareness horizon (bigger or smaller). If a space is too big to produce a clearly defined action (it produces a whole symphony of actions), it needs to be divided into smaller spaces to work with.**
2. **Find the action the space seems to be performing against the client.**
3. **If no clear result but charge is present, assess the list of action questions and take it from there.**
4. **Run the impact the space has on the client; use the client's description.**

4a. If the space performs no action but the client himself performs one that is related to the space, run it immediately and include "spot the space's resistance" in the instructions (a variation of step 5, skipping step 4).

5. **Run the client's counter-action as a complete DEEP Package.**
6. **Run the space as a viewpoint if no complete release.**
7. **If still no complete release, check for amplifiers (entities, family members, group minds...) and run their DEEP Packages against that of the client.**
8. **If there is still charge on the space, check flows 2, 3 and 4. The space in question must play a role in the drama. Run charged DEEP packages of all relevant viewpoints involved.**
9. **In later sessions, follow up on any charged subjects, incidents or character clashes uncovered while working with that same space.**
10. **When the work on one space has concluded, discuss with your client if he wants to formulate any policy or plans how to deal with that space in real life. Have him write it up and keep it for future reference.**
11. **Repeat steps 1-10 with other charged spaces until no more charge related to spaces.**

NOTICE: ATTENTION must be paid to breakthrough wins that require a longer period off processing.

DEEP Space Clearing is the DEEP program that is most closely related to the client's present time existence – the others tend to deal much more with his past. If a client suddenly gets a grip on some space that he had trouble accessing, this may result in a flurry of activities to work with this space, re-own it, upgrade or re-structure it etc. etc. During that time the client may not be interested in more sessions, even though the program is incomplete. He may be totally fascinated by and focused on the space he just recovered, and have no free attention for anything else. It is important to grant him all the time he needs to apply his inner-world session wins to his outer world too.

Appendices

Definitions for Deep Awareness and Aspect Clearing

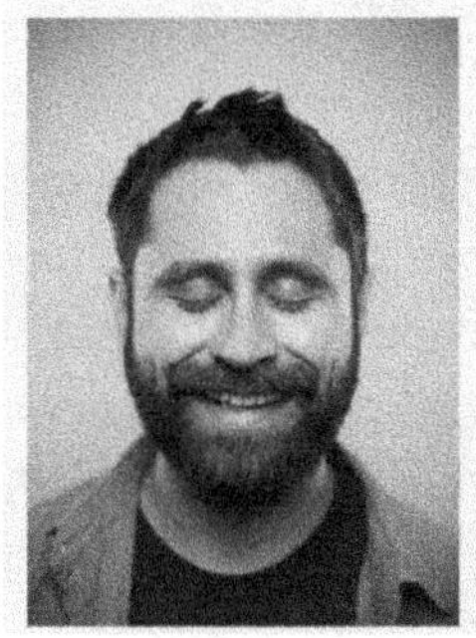  ***"You look into your body and sense how it feels inside. It may take a minute or so to really get in touch with what is there."***	**Deep Awareness:** (1) It is about *"how you feel inside"* when you think of a certain problem. (2) It could be called the *body awareness* of an issue or situation. It consists of all the subtle things that are going on in the body and energy body, rather than in the mind. (3) A feeling or energy in your body connected to a certain situation or issue. When a person sits quietly while concentrating on the issue, he/she can find these energies in or around the body. It can be in the form of emotions, feelings, pictures, tensions, impulses, masses, shapes, flows, etc. It may take a minute or so to develop and fully reveal itself. This is because we are contacting material we have totally forgotten about. We may have denied, suppressed and fought it. Simply allowing it to flow and accept it releases this charge; It completes its cycle of action when allowed to do so. *The Deep Awareness is the raw material of Aspects.*
 ***"You describe in words what you find. You are looking at a strange world of feelings and perceptions. 'Is it fantasy?' 'Am I just making it up?' you may ask. But No! It's your inner world that desperately wants to speak to you."***	**Aspect:** (1) The part of us that holds the negative reaction. (2) The state and condition of the energy body in response to a certain issue. It can be seen as a stuck identity consisting of subtle energies and behavioral patterns. (3) A part of us or a sub-personality that seems to have a life of its own. It exists below the consciousness level. An Aspect may express itself as irrational emotional impulses and reactions, including fear, anxiety or anger not called for; also as feelings hard to describe, masses and tensions. **Aspects are typically formed in moments of puzzlement, upset or overwhelm**. In hindsight *you find them by looking for stuck moments related to the issue.* If you think of an upsetting situation and look inside in your body, you will sense all these tensions, impulses, body-sensations and feelings connected to the situation. (See also Deep Awareness).

<table>
<tr>
<td>

Item: something personal,
sometimes weird. But it
represents the Aspect and
how it feels to the person.

"Here is the fun part: You express it as a symbol or 'thing'. Now you can move it around; you can speak with it. Soon you will become friends. It wasn't that bad after all."
</td>
<td>
Item: (1) It is the descriptive name or label we put on an Aspect.

(2) A representation of how the energy body feels, behaves and reacts regarding a certain issue.

(3) This is the name, description or symbol we give an Aspect. The Item can be a mental picture of ourselves in a certain situation; it can be a more abstract shape, picture or symbol; or it can be a mental shape or picture of a person we dealt with. It can also simply be an energy or mass in the body, such as a nervous stomach or a stiff neck.
</td>
</tr>
</table>

Visual Guide to DEEP and DEEP Aspect Clearing

Emotional Activities

Emotions are traditionally seated in the heart. But as you can see from the scientific study above, they spread throughout the body. We have a range of well-known and named emotions, such as apathy, fear, anger, boredom and joy. But beyond that there is a near infinity of *feelings* that are hard to describe but still very meaningful.

In *Deep Awareness and Aspect Clearing* we see emotions and feelings as guiding systems. They tell us important things about ourselves, about other people and situations in general – danger, neutral, opportunity, etc.

Feelings and emotions can however take over if ignored for a long time. They may take control over our mental activities and our body. Sometimes this can cause hell.

Deep Awareness and Aspect Clearing addresses the whole range of emotions and feelings and restores our emotional life to being a life quality and a reliable guiding system.

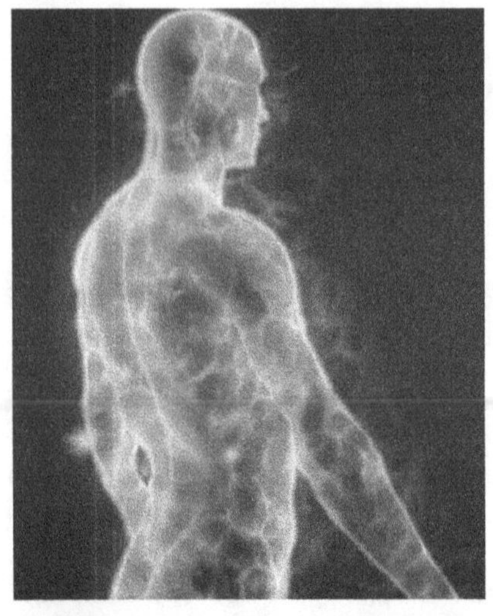

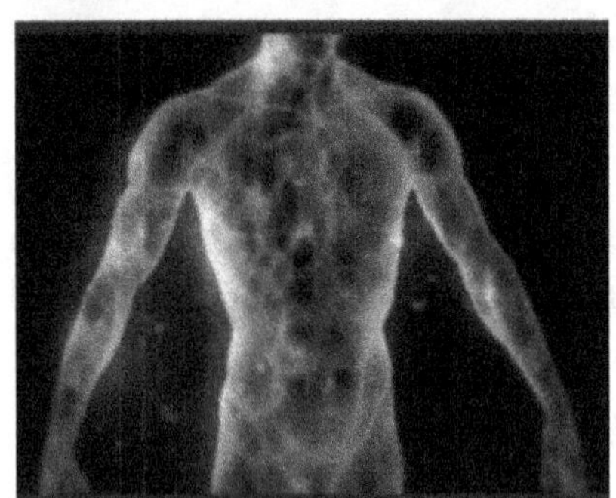

Body Activities (Physical Activity and Sensations)

The person's physical energies and body sensations are controlling and monitoring the body. Such energies can be sensed in the muscles and tissues in the activated parts - both as muscle activities (including impulses) and sensations.

Physical activity can be action and efforts, tensions, a state of rest, movements and whole routines. It can also be impulses that are precursors to physical actions and efforts. For some persons these 'non-physical efforts' are very important to include.

There is a range of body sensations such as: pain, hunger, fullness, soreness, pressure, exhaustion, a feeling of relaxation and wellness, etc.

Body activities also include what is called *body language*, consisting of posture, tensions, position of limbs, hands and head, facial expression and so on.

How we feel in the body obviously affects our sense of wellbeing and energy level in general. The energies and sensations that exist in the body at any given moment are of course partly due to our immediate or recent physical activity and our health. But many negative body sensations are rooted in what we call *Body Memories* stemming from long gone periods of physical, emotional and mental stress.

Such tensions can be located and relieved with Deep Awareness and Aspect Clearing.

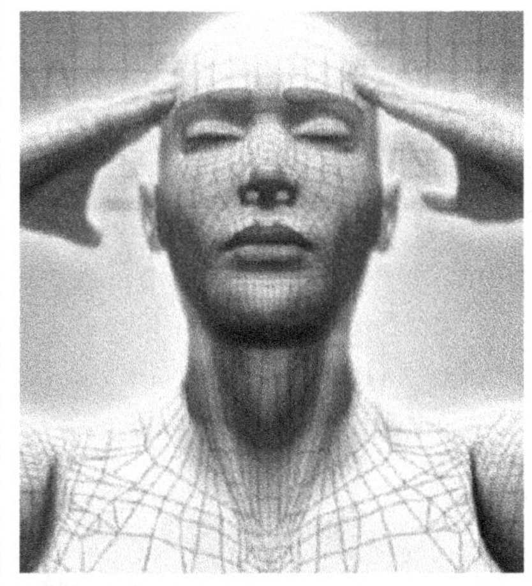

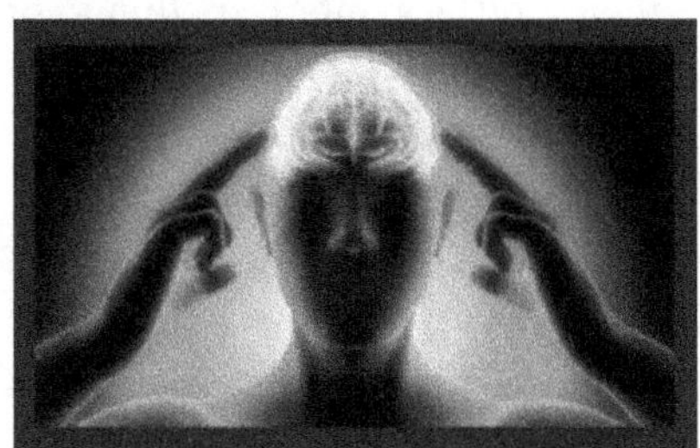

Mental Activities

Mental activities, such as thoughts, decisions, intentions and attentions, rational thinking, etc., are traditionally seated in the head. They include the use of language – be it written or verbal descriptions and messages sent and received.

Science shows they are concentrated in the head and brain, especially in the prefrontal cortex ('the Executive brain').

We may add that *you as a spiritual being are in control of the brain.* You *can* be in control of your attentions, intentions, thoughts and decisions.

Mental energies: thoughts, decisions, intentions, attentions, etc. may trigger responses in emotions and body. They may trigger negative or burdening reactions and sometimes keep them in suspense for a long of time.

In Deep Awareness and Aspect Clearing *we look into the interaction between head, heart and body and bring out and neutralize the reactive thoughts that may cause unnecessary distress and hardship.*

Deep Awareness and Aspect Clearing (DAC)

In *Deep Awareness and Aspect Clearing* we have the person contact these subtle energies and we do techniques and exercises with them.

It may take a little time (a minute or so) to contact these subtle energies that tend to take over in stressful situations. Especially emotional energies and body energies (including sensations) are prone to be out of control in many situations.

We have the person give a subjective description of the inner experience. Like, *"How does it feel in the body? Can you describe that in words?"* We then find a symbol, a 'thing' or image that would represent that.

Now we do a series of techniques and exercises that enable the person to get familiar with, release or gain control over these subtle energies. Doing this will eliminate negative and out of control factors. These factors sometimes seem so strange to us that they may be seen as destiny, curses, haunting spirits, being possessed, or sub-personalities.

The end-result of doing Deep Awareness and Aspect Clearing *is a harmonic state: emotionally, mentally and physically. There are no more stray sub-personalities or attachments that mysteriously pull you in the wrong direction. You are in control of your destiny.*

It is a state of integrity where you remain balanced and your own good self – even under trying circumstances.

"Visual Emotions"

Study Published by National Academy of Sciences, USA, 2013.

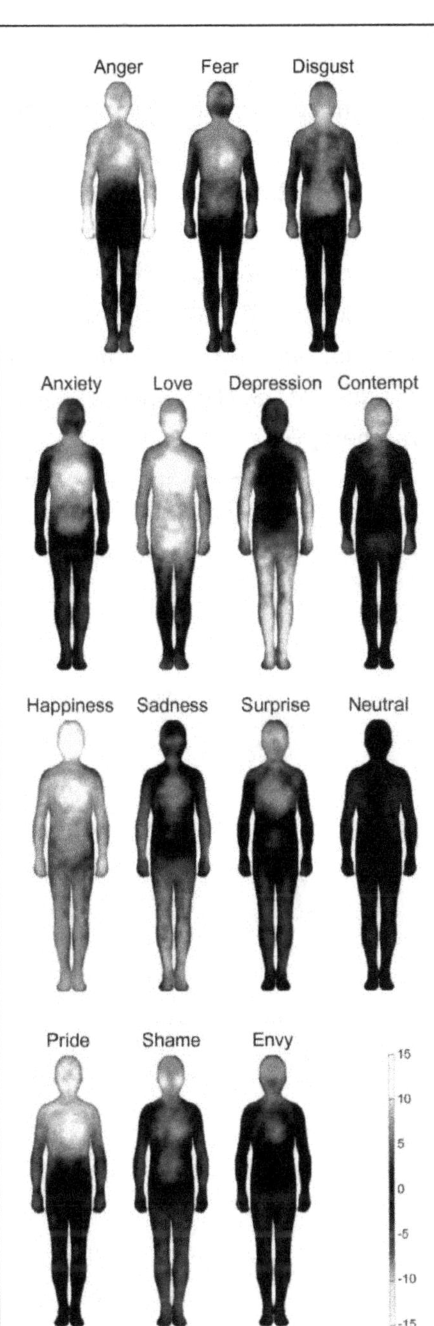

Body Maps of Emotions

From a scientific study done in Finland, 2012. Published by National Academy of Sciences, USA, 2013.

The Body Maps of Emotions
show various emotions and how their energies affect our bodies.

A university study was done in Finland with 701 participants. The subjects were Finns and Swedes – both peoples are known to be very formal and unemotional by the way. The subjects were exposed to emotional material, such as artwork, movie clips and short descriptions of emotional situations (descriptions like: 'a dying child in hospital' or 'a happy occasion of going to the beach with the family'). The participants were then told to depict where the resulting emotions showed up in the body. The warm colors show high activity. The cold colors show low activity to numbness.

See the 'thermometer' bar in lower right side of the table.

(Abstract)
(Emotions are often felt in the body, and somatosensory feedback has been proposed to trigger conscious emotional experiences. Here we reveal maps of bodily sensations associated with different emotions using a unique topographical self-report method. In five experiments, participants (n = 701) were shown two silhouettes of bodies alongside emotional words, stories, movies, or facial expressions. They were asked to color the bodily regions whose activity they felt increasing or decreasing while viewing each stimulus. Different emotions were consistently associated with statistically separable bodily sensation maps across experiments. These maps were concordant across West European and East Asian samples. Statistical classifiers distinguished emotion-specific activation maps accurately, confirming independence of topographies across emotions. We propose that emotions are represented in the somatosensory system as culturally universal categorical somatotopic maps. Perception of these emotion-triggered bodily changes may play a key role in generating consciously felt emotions.)

	(From: PNAS, November 27, 2013 PNAS = 'Proceedings of the National Academy of Sciences of USA' has been published since 1915, covering an extensive range of scientific subjects. It is the official journal of this highly respected scientific academy.) **(The article "Body Maps of Emotions" was submitted by** Lauri Nummenmaa - a,b,c,1, Enrico Glerean (a), Riitta Hari (b,1), and Jari K. Hietanen (d) Study was done under: Department of Biomedical Engineering and Computational Science and Brain Research Unit, O. V. Lounasmaa Laboratory, School of Science, Aalto University, Espoo, Finland; Turku PET Centre, University of Turku, FI-20521, Turku, Finland; and Human Information Processing Laboratory, School of Social Sciences and Humanities, University of Tampere, Finland.)

Unblocking and DEEP Subject Clearing

In DEEP Subject Clearing we combine the action of Unblocking (see below) with the tools in the DEEP tool box. Using the unblocking buttons we uncover charged elements. These elements are then fully discharged using the DEEP tools.

The unblocking buttons by themselves are designed to get the introspector to really duplicate and look into a subject. Let's say a person has all kinds of reactions to cats. A characteristic of a charged subject is that we cannot simply comfortably look at and duplicate what is in front of us. Instead of looking at a cat for what it is, the person in our example meets 'cats' with all kinds of defensive actions and attitudes; with a wide variety of emotional responses, reactions and thoughts.

The unblocking buttons are designed to get the person to look at all these bypass mechanisms and pop-up ideas and clear them away on a mental level. Once all these bypass reactions and repressions are cleared out of the way, the person can simply look at and duplicate 'cats' without all the irrationality and commotion. In normal unblocking this is accomplished by back and forth communication. The clearer asks questions, the person simply answers. In DEEP Subject Clearing (DSC) we take it a step further. We take up and clear the underlying DEEP packages and items. To do DSC the clearer has to be familiar with the DEEP tools, of course. They are used in the same way as in DEEP Incident Clearing and other main actions.

Below is described the normal procedure for unblocking. Then we describe the additional step of DEEP Subject Clearing.

In training, DEEP Subject Clearing is considered an easier subject to learn than DEEP Incident Clearing. So DSC is a good starting point for new trainees once they have learned Repeat and Tell and other basic DEEP tools.

Unblocking

Unblocking is a technique where we use a series of button questions to expose all aspects of a subject. It can also be used to repair a session that somehow went off the rails. This is called a Repair. **Each button question is asked repeatedly to get all possible answers**. When there are no more answers, we move onto the next question and use it the same way. If we unblock the subject of 'cats', the first question is, "On 'cats,' has something been suppressed?" As another example, question (4) 'Careful of' is: "On cats, is there something someone has been careful of?"

The questions are formulated in this open-ended way. A question does not define 'who is doing what to whom.' Anyone and any way it comes to the introspector's mind is valid. The important thing is to get the person to talk about the subject any way possible. If the person cannot see an answer in an area where there most likely is one, the clearer may poke around a bit, such as saying "have you suppressed anything on cats?" "Has your mother suppressed anything on cats?"—say just enough to cover the obvious. **Each question is asked repetitively until the person runs out of answers or has an endpoint for that button.** Then the next button is taken up. This is kept up until a full endpoint for the overall action occurs or the button list is finished. In the shown version there are 28 Buttons. Other versions exist and can be used. Once a question is embarked upon, the clearer has to make sure to use the same question to get another and another answer until the introspector says, there are no more answers.

1......has something been suppressed?

2......has someone expressed their opinion?

3......has something been invalidated?

4......is there something someone has been careful of?

5......is there something someone didn't say?

6......has something been denied?

7......has someone's communication been cut off?

8......is there something someone has been angry about?

9......has there been a conflict?

10....has a mistake been made?

11....has something been protested?

12....has someone had a grudge?

13....has someone been mocked or ridiculed?

14....has someone had a worry?

15....has something been decided?

16....has something been avoided?

17....has something been abandoned?

18....has something been finalized?

19....has something been ignored?

20....has something been insisted upon?

21....has something been pretended?

22....has there been a lack of help?

23....has something been misunderstood?

24....has something been altered?

25....has someone or something been resisted?

26....has there been a failure?

27....has someone or something been rejected?

28....has something or someone been helped

Normal unblocking, without the DEEP step added, is used as a repair tool. We can unblock items like a situation at work, a bad day with the children, a session that didn't go well, etc., etc. When a person is upset or worried about something and out of balance, it is a better idea not to use the DEEP step as we want to cover as much ground as possible lightly rather than go for an in depth handling of just one aspect.

DEEP Subject Clearing (DSC)

When the student clearer is comfortable with doing normal unblocking and using the DEEP tools, DSC is an easy combination of the two.

First you ask a button until no more answers, like in unblocking. Mark DEEP items in your worksheet as you go along. If an obvious DEEP package shows up you can however take it up right away. You have found some charge. Once that is handled, you can move on to the next button. If nothing obvious, you can quickly review the marked answers given for that button and maybe ask into one that has potential underlying charge. If nothing in particular is found, you move on to the next button.

You take up any DEEP elements, be it self-limiting or repressed thoughts, emotional content, or physical/effort content. Also charged persons can be taken up. If a charged emotion, effort or thought shows up it is dealt with using Repeat and Tell. As explained in Tools you cover in turn thought-emotion and effort of the DEEP package. An irrational thought could be taken up with Repeat and Tell; then accompanying emotion and effort are checked for and cleaned up if present.

Deep Incident Clearing, Light

This method can be used to release known traumatic or stressful incidents, like losses, accidents, break-ups, major upsets, past illnesses etc. We find the incident from the person's past and can then run it. First we check if the person is interested and willing to take it up, then we start to run it.

0. "Are you interested in running...?"
1. Locate the incident when (you fell off the bicycle.)
2. Where was it?
3. When did it happen?
4. Go to that incident.
5. How long does it last?
6. Go to the start of the incident and tell me when you have done so.
7. (Close your eyes) what are you perceiving (in the incident)?
8. Go through the incident to the end and tell me what happens as you go along.
9. Tell me what happened? (Ask only, if not already told.)

A. Go to the start of the incident and tell me when you have done so.
B. Go through the incident to the end.
C. Tell me what happened.

We run A,B,C, one or more times until the story has settled. Now we go into DEEP mode:

DEEP Mode (Subjective experience)

D1. Go to the start of the incident and tell me when you have done so.
D2. Go forward in the incident, and find the first moment of emotion, reaction or charge.

(We handle the DEEP package per below.) Then:
D4. Go forward from there, and find the next moment of emotion, reaction or charge. For each Moment (DEEP package), we have the person tell about the *subjective content*, question by question. "At that moment, are there any: 1.emotions? 2. feelings? 3. body sensations? 4. body language or posture? 5. actions or reactions? 6. impulses? 7. thoughts?"

Keep it light; just ask one after the other and have the person tell about it. For a charged category we can make a list and ask the person to sort out the dominant elements. We can ask the person to assign a number value to each (0-10). Just take what the person gives. Allow the person to look, experience and feel – and to talk. In this fashion the person reviews and sorts out the subjective elements of that DEEP package. Then we use the D4 instruction and find the next DEEP package. In this way we cover the whole incident. When that is done, we may use D1 and make a second – and maybe additional passes the same way until it is free of charge. We can then use "Other Points of View" below. In conflicts it handles the counter-force, a common cause of hang-ups. In DIC Light we do not always do so.

Other Points of View (POVs)

P1 Assume the viewpoint (VP) of (opponent.)

P2 From that VP, go to the start of the incident.

P3 From that VP, what do you see or perceive?

P4 From that VP, go through the incident to the end.

P5 From that VP, what happened?

We can also use DEEP mode on the other viewpoint. It can run much lighter.

When all is done, we can ask for another traumatic or stressful incident.

Alternative Method

1. You run the incident per 1-9 once and A-C until settled.
2. Now you tell the person: "Create a ball or container"
3. "Put all what you saw felt and experienced in the incident inside that ball"
4. Do Six Directions on the ball, maybe 3 rounds.
5. Ask the person to look into the ball and ask in turn:
6. Inside the ball, are there any: 1.emotions? 2. feelings? 3. body sensations? 4. body language or posture? 5. actions or reactions? 6. impulses? 7. thoughts?"

TOOL BOX

A collection of simple techniques that are used as part of a main action. The clearer who knows his/her business knows when to use a certain tool. Each tool has a special function and is used to accomplish one little step in a main action.

Repeat and Tell:

You have the person perceive and feel the DEEP element as deeply as possible. The person observes and accepts the phenomena as an energy in the body-mind system; that is the Repeat part. The perception of the pure energy can discharge it very quickly as this charge appears to be a sort of static electricity.

The Tell part is to invite the person to tell whatever comes to mind (pop-ups) in the form of thoughts, pictures, memories etc. This helps to understand the context and integrate it as a learning – as life experience. "Sense it as deeply as you can – if something comes to mind, tell me about it", is the format.

Repeating (of Thoughts, Decisions)

When it comes to running thoughts and decisions we start out with an answer that expresses the thought stemming from the repressed mind.

We take the statement and first we run it plainly, instructing the person to say it once as he really means it and then await an acknowledgement before he says it again. We have the person say it a number of times, each time it is acknowledged by the clearer. When this has run its course, the clearer asks the person to say it in different moods. The clearer may pick likely moods from the emotional scale, starting with likely low moods. Usually a statement gives meaning in some moods but not all. The trick is to see a scenario where it does make sense to say it in the mood picked. What often happens is that we hit a tone that really draws 'blood' – or at least charge. The same statement can be charged in several moods. An explanation could be that the thought has been used in many situations as a thought from one's basic arsenal. In other words the statement discharges when we hit these moods and this discharge is a valuable bonus. We start low and work our way up the moods – often ending up in humor.

Also, especially when it comes to command phrases or Dictates (statements adopted from other people in a traumatic incident) it is of great value to identify the likely source of the Dictate and have the person say it from that viewpoint, "As your father, say 'you must do your homework – or else…!'" could be an example.

Three –times-Solid (3xSolid)

You take a DEEP element, an identity or incident that is intangible or sometimes stuck and unmovable. You say "Make it more solid" 3 or more times; then "Hold it still" 3 or more times; then "Keep it from going away" 3 or more times. This routine makes the element more real and gives the person a sense of control over it. It can be used instead of Six Directions (see below) when the person seems unable to do the moving around of an item or incident. (From DEEP Character Clearing.)

Six Directions (6-D)

You take a DEEP element or incident that is intangible, stuck or 'unmovable' and put control in on it. "Place it above you"; "Place it below you"; "Place it to the right"; "Place it to the left"; "Place it in front of you"; "Place it to the back of you". In this way you move an item around that previously existed in the subconscious and exerted control over you. You simply take control instead of it taking control over you.

If you do 6-D on an incident you can ask the client to "create a ball or container". "Put everything related to the incident in that ball". Then you do 6-D on the ball. (From Robert Ducharme's R3X.)

Three Discharge Techniques

1-Have the person connect the center of the body to the earth through the feet. Also have the person connect to the 'higher up' – be it to a higher self, a religious figure or God. Connected in this way, have the person sense the item in question. 2. The person can also 'shine a yellow or white light into the energy (charge). 3 The person can be asked to expand and dilute the energy (charge), make the area bigger.

These are 3 ways of releasing the energy. The 3 tools can be used one alone or in combination. (From Science of Releasing by Marc Rüedi.)

Fixed Ideas

In addition to Repeating and using different moods and viewpoints in handling thoughts and decisions, we have Fixed Ideas handling. 1. If a fixed idea won't release easily, try the following. Ask "To your mind, what is the opposite to Idea A?" (Answer: Idea B.) Then: "Get idea A. Get idea B" back and forth to unstick the thinking. (From Frank Gerbode's Applied Metapsychology.)2. You can also use "How has idea A helped you? How has idea A harmed you?" back and forth. (From Heidrun Beer DEEP Manual.)

Before/After a Stuck Moment

"Recall a moment before the incident/stuck moment." "Recall a moment after the incident/stuck moment" done repeatedly can unstick shocks and the similar. (From Robert Ducharme's R3X.)

Dialogue or Hello/OK

1. The routine can be used in many contexts – to handle polarities, unfinished business, old conflicts, etc. Whenever you see two poles, be it persons, groups or phenomena in opposition, consider using this technique. (Marian Volkman of TIR. Originally from Fritz Perls', Gestalt Therapy.)

2. Can be done between 2 items/identities and between the client and an item/identity. Used to improve the communication between the parties – or develop a communication to resolve a conflict or polarity. First we do a few rounds of Hello-OK between the two sides. This establishes a communication line along which the messages can travel. It can be run this way:

As (item 1), say Hello to (item 2).	As (item 1), is there s/t you want to say to (item 2)?
As (item 2), receive that communication.	As (item 2) receive that.
As (item 2), say Hello to (item 1).	As (item 2), is there s/t you want to say to (item 1)?
As (item 1) receive that communication.	As (item 1), receive that, etc.

We use the forms like "As item 1 (e.g. your name)" and "As item 2 (e.g. your mother)" in order to put some distance between the items and the spiritual Being. Both the client's personality ("your name") and the item ("your mother") are creations of the Being – but not the actual person or mother by him or herself.

Alternate Confront

1. What part of [item] could you confront?

2. What part of [item] would you rather not confront?

Theory: This is a great little tool. It can be used on anything the introspector finds difficult to confront. For example, if one of the other tools hasn't worked all the way, try Alternate Confront. When asked for something he/she would rather not confront, the person still has to take a peek and identify it so the technique is all about confronting.

Note: "Confront" in the meaning used here is a receptive action. Synonyms are: duplicate, facing, inspecting closely, observing with Mindfulness and Witnessing.

Unblocking as a Repair Tool

Unblocking can be used as a repair tool. (See separate write-up in book). If a session or action seems to go nowhere and the clearer doesn't know what went wrong, doing unblocking on the session or action can loosen things up. The introspector is made to look at the session problem from many different angles. This helps get any charge off the situation. Sooner or later the team will find out what went wrong and the clearer can now correct it. When Unblocking is used in repair you don't run DEEP packages. Just let the person talk it out.

Fresh Reality (Grounding)

This is a class of techniques that helps the introspector become alert and grounded again when the going gets a bit tough in session. Symptoms like grogginess, sleepiness and the like, point towards the need for using Fresh Reality. It is also routinely used at the end of the session to get the introspector extroverted and back in the present again. It can be used in the middle of session after an action is completed with a proper end point. The clearer takes just one of the below lines and asks it maybe 10-20 times—until the introspector feels more alert and present.

Choose one line and ask it 10-20 times:

- *"Look at that (room object)", vase, table, picture, wall, etc., etc.*
- *"Pick a random object in sight." "How could you make that object more interesting?"*
- *"Point out something."*
- *"Where is the (room object)?" (introspector points.)*
- *"Look around here and find something you would like to remain in place."*
- *"Point out something in this room you could keep looking at."*
- *"What else is that (indicated object)?"*
- *"Duplicate something."*
- *"What is the condition of that (room object)?"*
- *"Find an object you are not in (inside)."*
- *"What scenario could (that object) be part of?"*
- *"Look around the room and find something that you like."*
- *"Look around and find something that is round."*
- *(You can use Round, Square, Rectangular, a certain color, etc. – any visual or even*
- *tactile characteristic, the point being to extrovert the attention.)*

GLOSSARY - DEEP

Aspect: (1) The part of us that holds the negative reaction. (2) The state and condition of the energy body in response to a certain issue. It can be seen as a stuck identity consisting of subtle energies and behavioral patterns. (3) A part of us or sub-personality that seems to have a life of its own. It exists below the consciousness level. An Aspect may express itself as irrational emotional reactions, such as fear, anxiety or anger not called for; also as feelings and body-sensations hard to describe, masses and tensions. Aspects are typically formed in moments of puzzlement, upset or overwhelm. In hindsight you find them by looking for stuck moments related to the issue. If you think of an upsetting situation and look inside in your body, you will sense all these tensions and feelings connected to the situation. (See also Deep Awareness).

Bypass mechanism: When the repressed mind is being triggered it means the rational mind has been bypassed. It is the mechanism of conditioned reflexes. It is automatic and fast but often overreacts or reacts on the wrong things.

Bypass Reaction: An Automatic reaction that bypasses the person's volition and control.

Charge: 1. Disturbing or harmful mental energy generated in mind and body. 2. Mental charge can be generated between conflicting viewpoints, ideas and mental objects in the mind. Charge is electrical in nature as it is generated between two poles—like between the plus and minus pole of an electrical battery. 3. Repressed, unfulfilled decision, emotion, feeling or effort. If a decision, emotion or effort becomes a completed cycle, the tension or charge ceases. If it is held back (repressed) or is stopped due to opposition, it still seeks to complete the cycle on a subconscious or unconscious level. This is what we call charge. When we in DEEP contact the DEEP elements and embrace and release them, the cycles are allowed to complete and the charge ceases to exist.

Clearer: the practitioner in DEEP; DEEP practitioner, sometimes called Life Coach.

D.E.E.P.: 1. An acronym that stands for Decisions; Emotions; Energies/Efforts; Polarities/Points of View. These are the elements of subjective experience. When found in the form of stressful mental recordings they are the elements of charge. They cover thoughts, emotions, sensations, physical behavior and experience and interpersonal conflicts and points of view. 2. DEEP Clearing, A method of self-improvement

Deep Awareness: (1) It is about "how you feel inside" when you think of a certain problem.

(2) It could be called the *body awareness* of an issue or situation. It consists of all the subtle phenomena and things that are going on in the body and energy body, rather than in the mind.

(3) A feeling or energy in your body connected to a certain situation or issue. When a person sits quietly while concentrating on the issue, he/she can find these energies in or around the body. It can be in the form of emotions, feelings, body-sensations, pictures, tensions, masses, shapes, flows, etc. It may take a minute or so to develop and fully reveal itself.

DEEP Character Clearing (DCC): A DEEP technique where we address archetypical identities and conflicts. We address identities or characters the person has been and identities or characters the person has fought. One identity (e.g. an opponent) is taken up and extensively processed. Then the client's own identity in the conflict is found and processed in a similar manner.

DEEP Element (DEEP Item): it can be a decision or thought, an emotion or feeling, an effort or impulse, a body sensation or perception. Each DEEP element exists as a recording that can be contacted and released by repeated mindful perception and talking about it. When we talk about DEEP elements we are talking about recorded (memorized) elements and not about thoughts and reactions happening in present time.

DEEP Incident Clearing (DIC): a main DEEP action where traumatic or stressful incidents are contacted and discharged. The story line of the incident is first sorted out. This may take several passes. Then we find and discharge the DEEP packages that are at the core of the traumatic or stressful content.

DEEP Package: A DEEP package is a moment of charge. It is one set of decision, emotion, sensation and effort. They were formed at the same time and make up a package of charge. The elements comprise four layers of the package. The DEEP package imposes a certain way of thinking, feeling and acting in an area. By clearing the package charge is removed and free life force is restored. Once you find one of the elements the other elements, if present, can usually be gotten by asking for them. The decision is the most important element to find; but all four layers should be contacted and discharged if available. You may start with asking for an emotion/feeling. You release that and ask for effort or impulse. You release that and ask for decision or thought. You release that and are done with that package. In other words, you start with the obvious DEEP element and then ask for the others.

DEEP Subject Clearing (DSC): this DEEP technique is used to discharge just about any subject the client can think of: "Fear of spiders", "being harassed at work", "trouble with the children", etc. We use a series of button questions to uncover DEEP packages related to the subject. Once they are in view, we use the DEEP tools to get all the charge off. DSC is often used as an exploratory action. Incidents, identities, etc. may be uncovered that can be further worked on using other DEEP actions and tools.

DEEP Toolbox: a collection of simple techniques that are used as part of a main action. The clearer who knows his/her business knows when to use a certain tool. Each tool has a special function and is used to accomplish one little step in a main action.

DEEP Viewpoint Clearing (DVC): a DEEP technique where charged incidents or relationships are handled by in turn viewing the matter from the viewpoints involved. Each viewpoint is handled as a DEEP package. Sometimes there are several packages related to one viewpoint. All packages found are handled with DEEP tools. DVC is especially suited for advanced clients where DEEP Incident Clearing may seem too tedious.

Dictate: 1. an automatic, uninspected thought that has command value. 2. A thought or decision coming from the repressed mind that has command value. It can be a self-limiting thought, an automatic response or other type of fixed idea. It fits under the category of thought and decision, but the word Dictate underlines that it has command value over the person.

End Point: 1. The positive conclusion of a DEEP action. The client is happy and the difficulty being addressed has been resolved. 2. The main actions of DEEP are always carried to an End Point. This is the point where a major positive change has occurred and the client has been released from the difficulty worked on. 3. There are various End points of techniques and actions. This is covered fully in Chapter 3 "Additional Data".

GPM: Goals-Problem-Mass. 1. When we have two opposing identities with opposite goals we have a problem that accumulates mass in the mind. They form a GPM. This kind of charge is addressed on DEEP Character Clearing*. 2. Archetypical problems that are built around conflicts between identities we have fought and identities we have been.

Introspector: 1. the person receiving DEEP clearing; client. 2. To introspect means to look inward. The introspector is continuously guided to look into his/her own mind, body and energy body in order to find the root causes to personal issues or difficulties.

Item: 1) It is the descriptive name or label we put on an Aspect.

(2) A *representation* of how the energy body feels, behaves and reacts regarding a certain issue.

(3) This is *the name, description or symbol* we give an Aspect. The Item can be a mental picture of ourselves in a certain situation; it can be a more abstract shape, picture or symbol; or it can be a mental shape or picture of a person we dealt with. It can also simply be an energy or mass in the body, such as a nervous stomach or a stiff neck.

Pop-up: any stray thought, association, incident, comment, etc. that pops up in the introspector's mind while reviewing something else. Usually the clearer simply listens, understands and acknowledges and returns to the action in progress. It is important to allow the introspector to talk freely about what pops up as it helps in dealing with the charge.

Repressed Mind: 1. The Repressed Mind is the repressed or never viewed part of the subconscious mind. It seems to have a will of its own. 2. That part of the subconscious mind that contains emotionally charged material and bypass reactions. It tends to bypass the rational mind and react directly to factors in the environment that are perceived as dangers. It is a collection of conditioned reflexes, of primitive survival patterns, that were "learned" during stressful and life threatening situations. It can be triggered by the environment when similar elements to the traumatic content are present. The Repressed Mind seems to have a will of its own in the form of out of control thoughts (dictates), emotions and impulses.

S/o: Someone.

S/t: Something.

Glossary for GPM Series

Note: For special terms in the GPM Series, use this special glossary. The GPM series was done based on some inspirational but incomplete research done by Ron Hubbard. DEEP Character Clearing is our attempt to complete this research of an important part of the case. We have used much of Hubbard's terminology which in general lies outside DEEP Clearing. Thus there is a need for this special glossary.

Auditing: self-improvement or therapy delivered in sessions.

Bank: The repressed mind. The traumatic part of the subconscious and unconscious mind.

Body Thetan (BT): A live, bodyless entity attached to a person's body. It is seen as a spirit in very bad condition (near spiritual death) that can be contacted, audited and released.

Clear: A major milestone in auditing where the person has overcome his bank or repressed mind.

Cluster: a group of body thetans held together by a traumatic experience.

Dianetics: Trauma and Incident handling therapy.

Dirty needle: A non-optimum needle reaction on the e-meter that indicates that a minor error has occurred in the auditing.

Dramatize: irrational behavior dictated by the repressed mind. Acting out behaviors dictated by trauma.

Dynamics: different spheres of life and the individual's urge to survive and succeed in that sphere. There are 8 dynamics: 1. Self. 2. Sex and family 3. One's groups. 4 Mankind 5. Animal kingdom and plants. 6. The physical universe. 7. Aesthetics and the spiritual universe. 8. Infinity and religion (God)

E-meter: Electronic instrument that reflects what happens in the client's mind. A bio-monitor.

Engram: Trauma containing pain and degree of unconsciousness.

Flat: A point where a technique produces no more change and therefore is ended.

GPM: A super-problem of goals and identities in conflict.

Grades: Beginning and intermediate auditing services, from grade 0-7-

Hubbard, Ron: (1911-1986) The developer and author of Scientology.

Key-out: A moment of release of charge; a moment of relief.

Line-plot: the pattern left in the mind of many conflicts that are stacked on top of each other; the underlying pattern of a GPM.

Lock: an incident where one is reminded of a more severe trauma.

OT: Operating Thetan. A high state of ability and awareness accomplished by doing the OT levels.

OT Levels: Advanced auditing levels. OT1-7.

Preclear: client

Pre-OT: Client on the OT levels.Theta: positive spiritual energy

Rock Slam: A needle reaction on the meter that indicates that something violent or destructive is found in the person's mind

Scientology: An applied spiritual philosophy. The central activity is to deliver auditing and do training to support that.

Secondary: Trauma containing severe loss such as loss of loved one.

Terminal: An identity, valence or beingness in the mind.

Thetan: the spiritual self, the soul

Valence: An artificial identity. A sub-personality.

Detailed Table of Content

www.ingramcontent.com/pod-product-compliance
Lightning Source LLC
Chambersburg PA
CBHW080845270326
41930CB00013B/3006
* 9 7 8 8 7 9 9 9 5 4 7 4 2 *